Victor Borge's
MY FAVORITE COMEDIES IN MUSIC

Victor Borge's MY FAVORITE COMEDIES IN MUSIC

by Victor Borge and Robert Sherman

DORSET PRESS
New York

This edition published by Dorset Press,
a division of Marboro Books Corp.,
by arrangement with Gurtman and Murtha Associates.

1992 Dorset Press

ISBN 0-88029-807-3

Printed and bound in the United States of America

M 9 8 7 6 5 4 3 2

Contents

Foreword

During interviews some of the more common questions asked are: who are your favorite composers? which are your favorite pianos, and favorite things in general such as, for instance, favorite intermissions?[1] This book may turn out as a kind of interview about my interpretations of and comments upon certain factual incidents concerning musical greats, and about unusual instruments I have met, and eccentric composers I'm sorry I haven't. You probably can't believe a lot of what you will read here, but try, because truth is not only stranger than fiction but a whole lot funnier. Schopenhauer wrote that humor overthrows logical expectations, and therein lies its appeal. I didn't have to invent any curious facts. It couldn't be simpler: So, to enable me to relate to you the ups and downs in the lives of the great masters, I just look them up and write them down. But if you are expecting a learned dissertation on polyphonic structure and things like that, you'd better find yourself another book, for this

---

[1] Advertisement for *My Favorite Intermissions,* the book preceding this one.

one is about laughter in the world of music, which I'd like to share with you. Believe me, musicians are just people. We have our ups, downs, and sideways. After all, all the super geniuses the world has known still got hungry, and could love and hate just like run-of-the-mill mortals. We certainly don't have to marvel any less at their artistic accomplishments just because we laugh a bit at incidents in their lives we find amusing. So read, smile, enjoy, and if you happen to learn something along the way, don't get upset.

V.B.

Introduction

One sunny day in the Garden of Eden Eve said to Adam, "Do you really love me?" "Who else," queried Adam tenderly, "could be my one and only?" With a deep sigh of happiness Eve beamed, "That's music to my ears!"

After the concert they went for a snack; but Adam wasn't hungry, and Eve had just a bite of an apple . . . and look at all the musicians that followed!

In no way has it been revealed which, or what kind of, musical selections the First Lady was listening to, but at least we learn from paintings depicting Biblical themes that it was played on harps, lyres, and trumpets, by angels on, above, under, or between clouds.

Later, of course, carvings and inscriptions on cave walls yielded further hints about living conditions including the gradual increase of noises as well as contraptions [1] with which to produce them.

From these clues it is fairly safe to assume that the forerunner of what thousands of years later would become

---

[1] Instruments

the clarinet [2] first appeared when a caveman blew into a blade of grass which he held between a couple of fingers. Envision—if you will—the man demonstrating his invention for his cavemate who, thrilled by the weird sound of each "pfipht" added a hearty "ha-ha." [3] Soon the entire community was waltzing "ha-ha"ppily along until the last straw was reached. [4]

With the introduction of the clariwhatnot, [5] the celestial trumpet, harp, and lyre, the slow progress of evolution began to demand a notch or two of musical discipline. It became necessary to find a method that would help the players produce the noises in a given order by organizing them in assigned registers and with precise intervals thereby making them systematically repeatable. Naturally, this called for musical compositions of which songs were the first and easiest kind since it didn't require other instruments beyond the human voice. But hardly had the first song been composed before someone invented singing it out of tune.

And that's what this book is all about:

The supreme masters who were forever being tripped by the unworthy around them, the immortals constantly held back by little people who thought they knew bet-

---

[2] As it was not a clarinet yet, we may call it a clariwhatnot.

[3] Both of them oblivious to the fact that they, in principle, had invented the WALTZ: "Pfipht, ha-ha, Pfipht, ha-ha", etc.

[4] Actually, a blade of grass, of course.

[5] See footnote no. 2.

ter. So many years have gone by that we can't really cry over the injustice of Brahms being ripped to shreds by some doddering critics, or Schubert being so poor that he couldn't afford to have his cracked eyeglass lenses replaced . . . and so on.

Let's laugh with the great ones knowing that in the end they triumphed—for they are the ones we love and remember, not the people who gave them the hard times.

Chapter One
A CASE FOR MUSICAL INSTRUMENTS

When I was a little boy in Denmark, I wanted to be a streetcar conductor. And now that I'm a bigger boy in America, I have given up the part that moves on rails. My career on the podium has been comparatively recent, because I didn't know I was going to live this long. What a thrill it is to get up in front of the New York Philharmonic, or any of the great orchestras, and almost be blown away by their incredible waves of sound. Like all conductors, naturally, I've had to study the different instruments,[1] and since it would be a shame to let all that knowledge go to waste, I decided to share some of it with you.

OFFBEAT INSTRUMENTS
Before we advance to the familiar instruments of the symphony orchestra, we have to remember that there are thousands of other soundmakers in use around the world, from *A*, which is a Korean percussion tube, to *Zeze*, a Congo-

---

[1] It can be terribly embarrassing to stand there scowling at the piccolos when the snare drum makes a mistake.

lese drum. There's a *Banga-Banga* and a *Bongo-Bongo,* not to mention the *Bingo, Bunga, Bonda, Bombo Bingy,* and *Bazoo.* It may sound like an auction, *going-going, gong,* but all of these are names of real instruments.[2] If you don't believe it, please look them up! (You don't have to bother, I already did.) [3]

MEET THE FAMILIES
Meanwhile, back to the symphony orchestra. Basically there are three types, or families, of orchestral instruments: the strings, which are plucked or scraped; the winds, which are blown or sucked; and the percussion, which are banged or bonged.[4] I'm not counting the keyboard instruments here, which are usually pressed or squeezed, because they don't usually figure in the normal course of orchestral events, and I have a whole chapter on the piano coming up in a little while.

STRINGS ALONG
I've always been partial to the string family because I used to play the violin before I took up the piano, and so did my father, who was in the fiddle section of the Royal Opera House in Copenhagen for thirty-five years.[5] Since there

---

[2] Would you be annoyed if someone presented you with a *Trumpeta Bastarda?*

[3] You don't get facts like these out of the Philharmonic program notes.

[4] There's also a group of instruments known as idiophones, but why add to the problems?

[5] When he finally came home, my mother hardly recognized him.

will also be a separate chapter on violins in this book, we can move right along to the violas, which are just like violins only bigger.[6] The cello stands about as tall as a 10-year-old boy,[7] so obviously it can't be tucked under the chin like a violin or viola. Instead, the player sits down and holds his cello between his legs, the bottom (of the cello, that is) braced against the floor with a short peg. Until about the middle of the nineteenth century, cellos didn't have pegs, and the musician had to hold the instrument off the floor by the pressure of his knees. This was changed by a Belgian virtuoso named François Servais, who grew so fat and tubby that he couldn't open his legs wide enough to grip the cello properly. His playing was getting worse and worse until he came up with the idea of making an end-pin that could be inserted into a holder at the base of the cello. The pin held the cello neatly off the floor, and Servais could have second helpings without worrying that he'd fluff the cadenza. Double-bass players have a different problem: their instruments are so huge that they have to play them standing up—or else perching on a high stool—to bow or pluck the bottom notes of the symphony.[8]

---

[6] There must be something else to say about violas, but I can't seem to think of it at the moment.

[7] Providing he's no taller than the cello.

[8] In 1889, John Geyer built a double bass that stood fifteen-feet high, but it never became popular. They probably couldn't find anybody tall enough to play it.

LUTE SALUTE

The stringiest string instrument in the orchestra is the harp, with forty-seven strings, but I like the guitar equally well. That's because the guitar, and its close relative, the lute, are not only among the most ancient of instruments, but the most romantic. After all, they have hourglass figures, a G-string, and they are always used for serenades. There's even an old South American legend which says that the guitar got its sexy shape because it was invented by a lonely gaucho, who carved himself a girl friend and made her sing soft sweet songs to him by caressing her on the pampas.[9] You have to take good care of guitars and lutes, and fuss with them to get the best results, but it's worth it.[10] As long ago as 1767, Thomas Mace wrote that the lute, being an especially sensitive little thing, should be "tucked into a Bed that is constantly used, between the Rug and the Blanket." There's one slight problem with this method, Mace admitted, therefore adding a warning that "no Person be so inconsiderate as to Tumble down upon the Bed whilst the Lute is there. I have known several Good Lutes spoil'd with such a Trick," he added. Franz Schubert actually did take his guitar to bed with him, and composed a lot of love songs there. He said it was the only place in the house warm enough to inspire him.

---

[9] How romantic can you get?

[10] Somebody once defined a lute player as a musician who spends half his life tuning, and the other half playing out of tune.

BRASSWINDS

Usually, musicologists talk about the woodwind and the brass instruments separately, but I'm in a hurry. Besides, except for the fact that the woodwinds are made out of wood,[11] and the brasses are made out of brass,[12] they really all make noises the same way: you blow into them and vibrate the airstream inside until something nice happens. Basically, there are three ways to do this. You can blow directly across an open hole with a resonating tube underneath it; you can vibrate your lips before blowing and sort of splutter into the thing, thereby becoming a direct part of the sound-producing process; [13] or you can do your blowing into a reed,[14] and leave the vibrating to us.

THE FLUTE

The modern orchestral flute, with all of its buttons and rings, is just a fancy version of the simple instruments pictured on cave walls. Primitive people would pick up a hollow stick and make sounds by blowing across the open end, the way kids will get tones by blowing across the top of an open soda bottle. Almost anything can be used for such simple flutes, including pieces of cane, animal bones,

---

[11] Except for some flutes, piccolos, bagpipes, etc.

[12] Except for some tubas, trumpets, saxophones, etc.

[13] Not to mention water-producing. Horn players get especially carried away with this part of the performance, which is why you always see them emptying their spit valves whenever they have a pause for a couple of measures.

[14] Remember the clariwhatnot?

dried fruit shells, even ostrich quills. An explorer named John Davis reported that Paraguayan Indians liked to make flutes out of the bones of missionaries. His book was entitled *Lectures from Paraguay Written by a Gentleman of Liberal Education and Considerable Property Who, Having Been Disappointed in his Hopes for Happiness with a Beloved Female, to Relieve the Distress of his Mind Resolved to Travel.*[15] In many cultures, people blow into flutes through their noses instead of their mouths. In addition to these nose flutes, you can find onion flutes, fipple flutes, lovers flutes, eunuch flutes, and conical bore flutes. In any case, the flute is the highest of the orchestral winds, unless you count the piccolo which is even higher. They're also the smallest, which is a good thing because you have to play them sideways, and the stage is usually crowded enough as it is.

THE CLARINET

Clarinets, like lawyers, have cases, mouthpieces, and they need a constant supply of hot air in order to function. As with the flute, there were many early forms of the clarinet. As long ago as 2700 B.C., the Egyptians made a kind of clarinet out of cane and the Romans made one that sounded more like a trumpet. They used to march into battle playing it, figuring the noise would scare the enemy half to death.[16] In India, they used a double-clarinet, which

---

[15] If he talked that way to the Indians, he's lucky they didn't bone and flute him, too.

[16] I bet it did, except when the wind was blowing the wrong way.

probably sounded twice as terrible.[17] It was primarily used for snake charming, since the snakes would do almost anything to get the Indians to stop playing it. In Sardinia they have a triple-clarinet.[18] Musicologists refer to these reed instruments as *idioglots,* but that's not very kind. I don't see them doing any better. The first modern clarinet was built by Johann Denner at the end of the seventeenth century, although his had only two keys, instead of the dozen or more you'll find on the present instrument. Other inventors came along and devised different variations of the instrument, but most of them didn't last. I mean, if you were Benny Goodman, would you want to play a riff on the *Glicibarifone* or the *Bathyphon,* or even the *Sextklarinette?* Today, the clarinet doesn't scare anybody, it just pleases us with its smooth, mellow tone.[19]

THE TRUMPET

The first trumpets sounded so horrible that they scared people out of their wits, which was precisely the idea. The ancients used trumpets as megaphones to frighten evil spirits or to signal special religious or magical events.[20]

---

[17] And scared the enemy half and half to death.

[18] Don't ask.

[19] In 1978, the Earl of Harwood, director of England's National Opera, backed his car into a parked vehicle fitted out with a screaming alarm. Arrested for leaving the scene of an accident, the Earl explained to the judge that the alarm sounded just like the clarinet in the Mozart Serenade he was listening to on the radio. The judge must have liked Mozart, too, because the case was dismissed.

[20] See?

The early tribal trumpets were played only by men (in certain Amazon areas, a woman who happened to look at a trumpet by accident was immediately executed), and Egyptian soldiers used them as a signal of war.[21] Romans called their trumpets tubas, but they sounded just as horrible.[22] The Chinese used such long trumpets that the bell had to rest on the ground, and the Tibetans still use a trumpet that is sixteen feet long. It's called *dung*.[23] In the middle ages, people finally figured out that you could curve some of the trumpet tubing and fold it back into a kind of S-shape. It still sounded pretty ghastly, but at least it didn't take so long to get out of town. Gradually, other improvements were added, such as crooks,[24] slides, valves, and better mouthpieces, until at last we reached the shiny, bright-sounding modern trumpets, used so brilliantly in their compositions by Wagner, Strauss, and others.[25]

AND MORE
What would you like to know about the other brasswinds? The oboe sounds like a clarinet with a cold, but it's the instrument that the whole orchestra tunes up to. The French

---

[21] Plutarch said that the blare of an Egyptian trumpet was like the braying of an ass.

[22] "Horibilis," to be exact. Roman writers also called the sound "raucus, rudis and terribilis."

[23] My word of honor.

[24] No reference to the players intended.

[25] "The snarling of stopped trumpets," complained New York critic W. J. Henderson about Strauss's *Elektra*; and the "jarring discords settle down into shrieks and groans which spit and scratch and claw at each other, like enraged panthers." Oh well, back to the drawing board.

horn looks like this:

 and if it doesn't . . . it's not a French horn, and the English horn is neither English nor a horn. The German name for bassoon is "fagott," but remember to put the accent on the second syllable. The trombone is another odd-looking contraption, shaped something like a four-foot paper clip. The player changes notes by moving a huge slide in and out, and must therefore be careful not to clonk the musician in front of him.[26]

BANG BANG

The percussion family includes everything that you can thump, whack, bang, bong, clack, clonk, slap, or rap. The instruments range from the tiny finger cymbals of Egypt to the enormous kettledrums of India that are so heavy that they must be mounted on elephants. There are literally hundreds of varieties of drums and bells and gongs, and still composers are forever looking for new noise-makers, writing parts for whips and sirens, vacuum cleaners and pot covers, automobile brake drums, airplane propellers, and rocket noise (and roll). It was at the premiere of one of those modern works that a dignified, well-dressed listener suddenly raised his umbrella high in the air. Attached to the tip of it was his white handkerchief.

ANIMAL FARM

Before we move on to other musical matters, I have to point out, in all fairness, that it's not only contemporary

---

[26] The trombone is sometimes nicknamed the slush pump, but preferably not where the trombonist can hear it.

composers who have far-out ideas. In 1892, for instance, an Italian journal carried an announcement of an instrument called the *Catano*. It consisted of a wooden case, with rows of compartments into each of which was placed a cat, big ones to meow the low notes, kittens for the treble. The idea was that when the notes on the keyboard were pressed down, instead of a string being hit, as in the piano, a wire pulled the appropriate cat's tail. "To produce a chord," the inventor explained, "three keys are struck and held down firmly, unless a staccato effect is desired, in which case the opposite touch is applied." [27] A similar device was introduced by an American named Curtis, who announced a "Grand Vocal and Instrumental Concert" with no less than forty-eight cats in a Cat Harmonicon. According to the *Cincinnati Folio*, "the first number was 'Auld Lang Syne,' but the cats were excited to such fury that they forgot all lessons, paid no attention to time, tune, rhythm, or reason, and simply drowned the sound of the organ in an unearthly tornado of caterwauling. The men stamped with all their might and the platform came down. The cats darted in every direction, adding to the confusion, until there was a cry of 'Fire,' and the engine came and poured a deluge of water through the window, drenching the crowd immediately." It was also in Cincinnati, by the way, that an instrument called the *Porco-Forte* was introduced, operating on exactly the same principle as the Cat Harmonicon, except with pigs in the compartments instead of cats. "If the pigs are well selected," re-

---

[27] If you don't know what "staccato" means, don't worry about how the opposite touch is applied.

ported the *Musical World* of November 14, 1839, "they will wear about three years without tuning."

TA-TA

That's about all for now about musical instruments. Later you'll hear about pianos and violins, and if you prefer, I *won't* tell you about other gadgets that came along through the years like for instance, a patent for a musical bicycle, filed in 1896 by a man in Iowa who claimed it would encourage the riders to pedal faster. And a few years before that, a Frenchman invented a musical petticoat. "With the aid of a scientific mechanism," reported the *Boston Musical Times* of September, 1860, "the crinoline is inflated like a life-preserver. The elegant wearer need only touch a spring, and the air in her skirt sets in motion a musical attachment playing tunes from the gems of opera. The inventor declares that the ballroom orchestra may be entirely dispensed with in the future, since the ladies can now provide themselves with waltzes, quadrilles, and polkas to their hearts' content." [28] In other words, when you go to a concert you have to be grateful not only for the instruments that you do hear, but for the ones you don't. Or, as Shakespeare put it, "sometimes a thousand twangling instruments will hum about mine ears . . . that if I then had wak'd after a long sleep, will make me sleep again."

---

[28] A few years later, another Frenchman patented a musical bed. It figures.

Chapter Two
THE EARLY COMPOSERS

VERY EARLY COMPOSERS

First the good news: we don't have to worry about the very early composers. They mostly had funny names, like Walther von der Vogelweide and Oswald von Wolkenstein,[1] and since they spent most of their time serenading ladies while their husbands were away on the Crusades, they didn't actually have time to compose very much. Other early musicians did stay home quietly and write, but their lives were so dull they don't belong in this book. Hermannus Contractus was very big in the eleventh century, but no one cares much about him any more.

GOOD START

The first important composer was Guillaume de Machaut, who was born in France in 1300. He was considered a genius, but we don't hear very much of his music nowadays, because he didn't write symphonies or concertos or

---

[1] Not to be confused with David Wolkenstein, author of *Primum Musicum volumen scholarum Argentoratensium*.

useful pieces like that. He concentrated his efforts mostly on lays.[2] Machaut served at the courts of the King of Bohemia, the Duchess of Normandy, the Duke of Berry, the King of Navarre, and even the King of France, because it was much easier than working for a living. He also established a pattern that hundreds of other composers would follow, for only members of the nobility could afford to have musicians hanging around just in case they wanted to have a good tune with their supper.

ROYAL FLUSH
As various kings and queens started competing with each other to see who could have the most elegant court, more and more composers found that serving the nobility was not a bad deal. They would write music for horse shows and masquerades, for wedding processions and birthday parties, and maybe they'd play the lute during the queen's supper, or soothe the king to sleep with a tune on the viol. For all this, they got a nice salary, shiny uniforms, and were allowed to walk around with fancy titles like "Gentleman of the Chapel Royal, Keeper of the King's Closet," and "Master of the King's Band." Sometimes the composers got pretty intimate with the royal family. Orlando Gibbons was "Musician for the Virginalles to Attend in His Highness' Privie Chamber," Philip Rosseter was a "Child of the Revels of the Queen," and Nicholas Lanier was known as the "Keeper of the King's

---

[2] The medieval so-called lay was a lyrical poem set to music. You really ought to know that.

Miniatures."[8] Pretty soon it got to the point where royalty couldn't do a thing without somebody setting it to music. Even the royal physicians wouldn't attempt an operation without preparing the patient with appropriate music beforehand, and when the royal chefs prepared the aphrodisiac for the royal banquets,[4] they insisted that it be accompanied by the sensuous music of lute, vielle, or psaltery. Of course, if he wanted to douse the guests' amorous fires, the chef would call in the cornets and shawms, and serve up a salad laced with rosemary, fennel, and rue.[5]

ROYAL CLASH

Gradually, most of the best composers drifted to the various courts of Europe, so problems naturally arose between the monarchs (who expected complete obedience) and the muscians (who were proud of their cultural independence). In the early 1500s, the great Josquin des Pres had several times been promised a raise by his boss, Louis XII of France. Louis kept forgetting about it, though, and when his patience gave out, Josquin wrote a new motet to be sung before the king, using a section of the 119th Psalm: "Oh, Think upon the Word You have Given Thy Servant." He cleverly devised the music so that the phrase was repeated again and over again, to the

---

[8] One of his favorite songs was "Upon my Lap my Sovereign Sits."

[4] Asparagus and turnips cooked with chestnuts in cream was one popular dish.

[5] That would work for me every time.

point that, according to one chronicle of the period, "the king would have been exceptionally hard of hearing not to notice the hint thus conveyed to him." Anyway, he did notice, he smiled, and came through with the raise. Whereupon, Josquin wrote another motet on a different phrase from the same Psalm: "Thou Hast dealt Graciously with Thy Servant." [6]

ROYAL CRASH

But nevertheless, composers were servants and the best of them had to remember that fact, as Lully found out a couple of kings later. Lully was the most powerful musician in France, having convinced Louis XIV to grant him a total monopoly on producing operas in Paris. One day, though, the king sent a messenger summoning Lully for something or other, and the composer sent back word that he was busy and the king would have to wait. Well, the fur really flew. Louis was so furious [7] that he threatened to withdraw the composer's special favors, and at the very next court concert there was the king sitting in the first row, scowling like mad. Poor Lully did everything he could think of to get the king to smile, but nothing worked. He removed a scheduled work and replaced it with one of Louis's favorites; he even got up and played

---

[6] On another occasion, Louis asked Josquin to compose a piece in which the king himself might sing. Knowing the extent of the monarch's musical talent, Josquin prepared a complicated canon with an extra part for Louis that consisted of one single note, rather like "Night and Day," in the song by Cole Porter.

[7] Pun not intended!

the fiddle himself, but all he saw was more scowls. Finally, remembering the extent of the monarch's sense of humor, Lully rushed out from the back of the stage, ran right through the orchestra, and hurled himself onto the harpsichord, smashing it to pieces. The king burst into howls of laughter, and Lully smiled too, knowing that at last he was back in good graces.

ROYAL SQUASH

A similar situation occurred in England, where the renowned and revered Dr. Christopher Tye was not only "Gentleman of the King's Chapel," but organist to Queen Elizabeth. She once sent the verger to tell him that he had played out of tune that morning, whereupon the good doctor returned a message saying that it wasn't so. "It must have been Her Majesty's ears that were out of tune this morning," he said. That seemed entirely possible to Elizabeth, so she let the matter drop.[8] Another, much more dramatic clash between a composer and his boss involved the Italian violinist and singer Alessandro Stradella and a Venetian nobleman. The nobleman hired Stradella to give voice lessons to his beautiful fiancée, Ortensia, and before you know it, Stradella is teaching her other things as well. Eventually Stradella and Ortensia ran away together, and the nobleman was so upset that

---

[8] Despite all those dignified portraits you may have seen, Elizabeth was a very down-to-earth person. She swore a lot, drank beer, and danced five or six galliards for her morning gymnastics. She also kept saying she had nothing to wear because her wardrobe contained only three thousand gowns.

he paid two assassins to track down the composer and dispose of him. Sure enough, the ruffians followed the couple to Naples and then on to Rome, where Stradella was to sing the principal part in a new oratorio he had just written. The two villains went to the church to wait for the performance to finish, but were so overcome by the gorgeous music that instead of killing Stradella, they went up to him afterward, confessed the plot, and urged him to escape.[9]

BASICALLY BAROQUE

By the time the seventeenth century rolled in, music was no longer the exclusive province of church and court. Opera was being born, the sonata, concerto, and other new instrumental forms were becoming enormously popular, and there were vast improvements in the quality of the instruments themselves. This was known as the baroque era.[10] If you look up "baroque" in ten different encyclopedias, you'll get ten different explanations, all of them impossible to understand. The best I can do is to tell you that, according to the *New Dictionary of Music,* the term in the eighteenth century meant "uncouth, odd, rough, and antiquated in taste." How baroque! One big advantage of the period was that composers didn't have to

---

[9] I wish I didn't have to tell you the sequel to that lovely story. What happened, though, is that the nobleman, more furious than ever, simply went out and hired a pair of tone-deaf murderers who did the job properly.

[10] At least that's what we call it today. In those days, people didn't even realize that the Renaissance was over.

depend on royal favors any longer, if they didn't want to. They could write music for theaters, parties, funerals, and all sorts of other private and public occasions and, provided they didn't take too long about it, they'd make a pretty good living.

TIME FOR TELEMANN

First I must tell you about Georg Philipp Telemann, the fastest pen in the west. Handel, who knew him quite well, said that Telemann could toss off an eight-part motet as easily as anybody else could write a letter, and Georg Philipp himself was quoted as observing that "a proper composer should be able to set a placard to music." Telemann wrote music as if there were no tomorrow, and since he wound up with more tomorrows than most folks (he lived to be eighty-six), he probably wrote more music than any composer before or since. Telemann was born in 1681. When only a small child he learned to play the oboe, zither, flute, and violin, and he could already speak Greek and Latin. He was also quite fluent in German, but that was less surprising.[11] When Georg decided to become a musician his parents were shocked. Music was all right as a hobby, they felt, but it wasn't at all a proper career for a clergyman's son.[12] So the boy was packed off to a school in a lonely little town in the Harz Mountains, where he was supposed to study geometry and forget about music. Naturally, Georg got mixed up and forgot about geometry.

---

[11] I forgot to tell you that Telemann was born in Germany.

[12] I also neglected to mention that his father was a priest.

FIRST CHANCE

One day a music festival was scheduled to take place in the little town, and the man who was supposed to direct it didn't show up. Georg was only thirteen at the time, but he begged and pleaded for a chance to substitute, and since there wasn't another conductor to be found in the whole lonely Harz Mountains, Telemann got the job. What's more, he did it so splendidly that the local mountaineers carried him away on their shoulders, in triumph. Georg was now more determined than ever to become a musician, but as soon as his parents heard about his escapades, they sent him to another school in Hildesheim, to study logic. Georg soon started giving his parents very logical reasons why he should become a musician, so they yanked him out again and sent him to law school in Leipzig. They needn't have bothered, of course. Georg learned just enough law to realize that his parents had no legal hold over him anymore, and then he stopped discussing the matter. He simply moved to Hamburg and set up shop as a composer, just as he had wanted to do in the first place.

FIRST CHOICE

By this time, Telemann was so bursting with musical pieces his parents hadn't let him compose, that he became absolutely nutty about it. He wrote twelve funeral services and fourteen wedding services and twenty anniversary services, forty operas, forty-four oratorios, sixty overtures, hundreds of chamber pieces, and at least three

thousand songs.[13] He wrote Installation Music for the
Hamburg clergy, Captains' Music for the Hamburg sea-
farers, and Table Music for the aristocratic Hamburgers.
Several times, Telemann tried to prepare catalogues of his
music, but he always gave up because even he couldn't
remember all of it.[14] For years after he died, nobody
played a note of Telemann's music since it was too much
trouble to go wading through stacks and stacks of pieces
just to find the one they wanted. Nowadays, some people
aren't nearly so lazy, luckily.

VIVA VIVALDI

Although Telemann was from Germany, the real flood of
music in the early baroque period came from Italy, where
they invented the concerto. The first composers of concertos had names like Jomelli, Torelli, Corelli, and Locatelli, and their concertos sounded pretty much alike, too.[15]
In Italian, the word "concerto" means "the sounding together of separate parts" and Antonio Vivaldi was loaded

---

[13] Not counting the three volumes of fantasies, the forty-four pas-
sions, and a cantata called "Die ungleiche Heyrath oder Das
herrsch-süchtige Camer Mädgen!"

[14] In his spare time, Telemann wrote poetry, engraved scores, prepared a method book for singers and harpsichord players, and
completed his autobiography.

[15] See also Giardini, Agnostini, Bononchini, Gasparini, Sammartini,
Mancini, Tartini, Nardini, Turini, Pasquini, Sacchini, and
Schütz.[16]

[16] Never mind about Schütz. I just put him in for variation.

with parts, for he wrote more concertos than anybody else. Vivaldi was born in Venice, and nobody knows exactly when.[17] After approximately whenever, he lived and when he died, hardly anybody remembers when that happened, either. They don't even know for certain where. Some books say it was Venice in 1743, others claim it was Vienna in 1741. In between, however, Vivaldi became a famous violin virtuoso, a respected teacher, a prolific composer, and he even got to say Mass once in a while. Yes, Vivaldi was a fully ordained clergyman, often known as the "Red Priest" (because of his hair), although he gave up the ministry after a while. The story went around that every time he thought of a good fugue tune he would stop right in the middle of a service to run off to his studio and write it down. When somebody reported him to the inquisition, Vivaldi explained that it had nothing to do with fugues. He only rushed away from the altar that way, he said, because his asthma was bothering him.

SCHOOL DAYS
After his career as a priest fizzled, Vivaldi devoted all of his time to music. His main job was as a music professor at a convent school for illegitimate and orphaned girls in Venice, and since some of the girls were nineteen and twenty years old, Antonio often was in love with his work. The young ladies gave concerts every week, wearing

---

[17] *Groves Dictionary* says 1675, the *Ewen Encyclopedia* lists 1678, and in the *New Dictionary of Music*, it's 1685. Now, it's up to you.

white gowns and pomegranate flowers over one ear, and
it was all terribly romantic. The soloists were usually
known by their first names and the instruments they
played, like Cattarina del Cornetto or Michialetta del
Violino, and pretty soon all the eligible bachelors in
Venice were flocking to hear Tony Vivaldi and his All-
Girl Orchestra. A lot of them didn't care for music all
that much, actually, but it was fun to go backstage afterward and look at the instruments. Incidentally, it wasn't
considered dignified to applaud inside a school in those
days, so the men showed their appreciation by coughing,
shuffling their feet, and blowing their noses very loudly.[18]
Naturally, Vivaldi composed all sorts of pieces for the
girls to play, including concertos for mandolin, piccolo,
guitar, violin, cello, and trumpet. Some of his prettiest
pupils played the bassoon, so Vivaldi wrote thirty-nine
bassoon concertos for them. He started publishing his
concertos by the dozen, because it helped with the book-
keeping.

SPEEDY ANTONIO
Vivaldi composed with incredible ease. He once claimed
that he could write a concerto faster than the copyists
could take it down, and he proudly wrote "completed in
five days" on the cover of one of his three-act operas. Of
course, sometimes when he was in a hurry, he would
swipe tunes from his earlier works and use them again. If

---

[18] Come to think of it, there always are a couple of appreciative
guys like that at *my* concerts.

he couldn't find any of those, he would instead borrow tunes from other people's works.[19] One of Vivaldi's specialties was musical paintings, and in his concertos you'll find imitations of birds, crickets, sea tempests, and even chattering teeth. That's not bad for a red-haired priest who was born, we don't know exactly when, but at least three hundred years ago.

---

[19] In Vivaldi's *Rosmira*, musicologists have found bits and pieces from operas by Micheli, Paganelli, Pamino, Mazzoni, Hasse, and others. Good thing those other guys never went to Vivaldi's concerts.

Chapter Three
FRANZ JOSEPH HAYDN

Franz Joseph Haydn was born on March 31, 1732 (some books say April 1 but they must be fooling), in a little town along the Austrian-Hungarian border.[1] His mother was a cook, while his father combined the jobs of wagon-repairer, winegrower, housepainter, and village magistrate, which entailed keeping a sharp lookout for adulterers, gamblers, and people who didn't go to church on Sundays. He had to turn in a report on them every week. As a very small child, Joseph sang with an unusually clear and beautiful voice, so already at the age of seven he was in a church choir. He also learned to play the violin, the clavier, the kettledrum, and the tambourine, and sometimes he helped ring the church bells that announced services, thunderstorms, and other local disasters. He didn't like school much,[2] and he didn't get enough to eat, but what the heck, it was a living.

---

[1] It was either called Rohrau or Trstnik, depending on which side of the border you were coming from.

[2] According to an instruction sheet issued by the Town Council, the teachers were advised "to refrain from pulling out the hair of pupils, but to keep them strictly in order with the cane."

SING OUT

One day the choirmaster of Vienna's famous Saint Stephen's Cathedral came to town, heard Haydn sing, and was so impressed that he emptied a whole plate of cherries into the boy's pockets. "Whenever I hear a trill," Haydn used to say, when an old man, "I can still smell those cherries." He also asked that Joseph be allowed to return with him to Vienna, and there, at the age of eight, Haydn began his career as a choirboy. He worked hard at his music, singing, playing, and studying pieces by the most important Viennese composers of the day, people like Fux, Tuma, Ziana, Palotta, and Bonno.[3] When Haydn left the choir at the age of seventeen, he was thrown out for cutting off another singer's pigtail, he bummed around Vienna for nearly eight years more, doing odd jobs, playing at dances, singing at outdoor parties, and teaching.

NEAR MISS

One day he fell madly in love with one of his students, a lovely girl named Therese, but she was so shy that she ran away and joined a convent. Poor Haydn had to content himself with writing her an organ concerto, to show her what she was missing, and then he went and married her sister, instead. Was that ever a mistake! According to all the books I've searched, Maria Anna Aloysia Appollonia was ugly, unpleasant, quarrelsome, jealous, stupid, bigoted, wasteful, unable to bear children, unmusical, and a

---

[3] Not to mention Carl Ditters von Dittersdorf.

sloppy housekeeper. She kept pestering Haydn to do something more useful than writing music, and liked to use his manuscript pages to curl her hair with, or line the pastry dishes.[4] It was with Maria in mind that Haydn wrote a little song that went:

> If in the whole wide world
> One very worst wife there is,
> How sad it is that each of us
> Knows well that she is his.

HELP WANTED

If Haydn's marital life left a good deal to be desired,[5] his professional life was really looking up and in 1761 he accepted the position of Vice-Kapellmeister to Prince Paul Anton Esterhazy. The prince lived in a modest palace at Eisenstadt,[6] and he made Haydn sign a contract promising to be "temperate, mild and lenient, abstaining from undue familiarity and from vulgarity in eating, drinking, and conversation, taking care to be punctual, and practicing on all instruments that he is acquainted with."

---

[4] When Haydn called her "that infernal beast" he was thoroughly composed.

[5] Maria kept pushing her husband to buy her a little cottage to live in when she became a widow. Eventually Haydn did buy it, but moved into it himself, a merry widower.

[6] It only had two hundred guest rooms, and a picture collection that later became the foundation of the Budapest Museum of Fine Arts.

HELP NEEDED

It was quite a job. Haydn lived in the servant's quarters, right over the stables, and he was not only supposed to compose new music at the drop of the prince's command, but to serve as librarian, take charge of fixing the instruments, see that the musicians' uniforms were neat, help the copyists, give voice lessons, turn in attendance reports on the players, lead rehearsals, and conduct concerts. A year or two later, Prince Paul died and was replaced by his brother, Prince Nicolas Josef Esterhazy, His Serene Highness and Knight of the Golden Fleece, although you could just call him "The Magnificent." [7] When he took over, the court was still in mourning for his brother, so Nicolas only had them shoot off nightly celebration fireworks for the first few weeks. After a while, though, he got bored with Eisenstadt, so he took a swamp, had it drained, and built on it a fantastic new summer palace designed to outglamorize Versailles. He called it Esterhaz, so everybody would know who paid for it, and he had it outfitted with hundreds of rooms, connected by frescoed halls and lit by crystal chandeliers. There were flower gardens and game parks and hot houses and guest cottages. There was a hall of clocks with golden cuckoos, and a library of eight thousand expensively bound books. There was a marionette theater whose walls were studded

---

[7] Prince Nicolas owned 21 castles, 60 marketplaces, 207 dairy farms, and 414 villages (complete with serfs), and he liked to wear a jacket covered with diamonds. Otherwise, he was just one of the boys.

with seashells and precious stones, and an opera house where all the loges opened into sumptuous back rooms, luxuriously furnished with fireplaces, divans, and huge clocks.[8] The climate was foul, the location remote, and the bedrooms drafty, but the prince said he liked it, and that's what counted.

BUSY BODY

Meanwhile, here's Joseph Haydn, one of the greatest musical geniuses the world has ever known, putting on his wig and blue servant's uniform every morning, and patiently waiting in the prince's antechamber for the day's orders. Needless to say, whatever the prince wanted the prince got. A new opera for the puppets? Certainly. A new symphony for the empress? Of course.[9] Quartets, sonatas, masses, overtures, cantatas, marches, minuets—they named it, Haydn wrote it. He even had to prepare thirty pieces for the prince's mechanical clocks, and a thirty-first for a crazy armchair that played a flute-tune when you sat down in it. Eventually Haydn himself began to lose track of all his compositions, so he started giving some of them nicknames like bear, chicken, lark, frog, donkey, and emperor.[10] He swapped his "Razor" Quartet for a new set of shavers,

---

[8] When his guests were bored by the opera they could go inside, light the fire, sit on the divan, and watch the clocks for a while.

[9] When Marie Therese came to Esterhaz, Haydn not only had to prepare and conduct the new music, but run into the field and shoot some grouse for the royal dinner table.

[10] Not necessarily in that order.

and wrote the "Ox" Minuet for a butcher's daughter. When the courtiers fell asleep at his concerts he shocked them awake with his "Surprise" Symphony, when they talked too much at breakfast he invited them to "Der Kafeeklatsch," and when they complained about the weather he suggested, one hundred fifty years before Jerome Kern, "Wait Till the Clouds Roll By." [11]

FRIEND AT COURT

One thing that enormously brightened Haydn's life at Esterhaz was the arrival of an old violinist named Antonio Polzelli. All right: what really cheered Haydn up was the arrival of Antonio's pretty, nineteen-year old wife, a Neapolitan singer named Luigia. According to contemporary accounts, Luigia wasn't a very good singer [12] and the prince actually ordered his Kapellmeister to fire her, but somehow Haydn never quite found time to do it. He would look at Luigia's "deep, black eyes, chestnut hair, delicate figure and soft, peachbloom complexion," then run back and tell the Prince that she wasn't as bad a singer as all that. He also started to give Luigia long lessons to improve her singing, and he kept rewriting her arias to take out all the hard parts. That must have helped a lot for after a couple of years of lessons Luigia gave birth to a baby boy.[13]

---

[11] He also composed a symphony called "The Absent-Minded One," but I can't remember why.

[12] Something seemed to run in the family, for Antonio wasn't a very good violinist, either.

[13] They didn't call him Papa Haydn for nothing.

FRIEND IN VIENNA

When Haydn wasn't giving voice lessons to Luigia in Esterhaz, he was giving orchestral lessons to Marianna von Genzinger in Vienna, the main difference being that she had six children.[14] It was a perfect relationship. He gave her songs and sonatas, she gave him zwieback and ragout with little dumplings. "Oh the memory of those glorious days," he wrote of her, "all those wonderful evenings can only be remembered, but not described. How I long for the day to come when I shall have the inexpressible pleasure of kissing your hands a thousand times for so many wonderful things. . . ." [15]

BETWEEN GENIUSES

Another great good friend of Haydn's during this period was Wolfgang Amadeus Mozart. The two composers loved each other's music, played quartets together, and had fun teasing each other. There's a story about the time Mozart bet Haydn that he could write a piece that Haydn couldn't perform. Sure enough, when Haydn put the music up on the rack and began to read it through, he had to stop suddenly in the middle of a page; there was a single note to be sounded right in the middle of the keyboard at exactly the same moment that his right hand was busy playing the highest notes on the piano, and his left hand was needed for a chord in the bass. "Nobody can play that," grumbled

---

[14] But not with Haydn.

[15] "P.S.," he added, "Please give my respectful compliments to your husband."

Haydn, whereupon Mozart slid over on the bench to show
him how. When he reached that point in the music, he
simply leaned over and struck the extra note with his nose.
"You're right," Haydn conceded with a laugh, "but remember, with a beak like yours it becomes a little easier!" [16]

LONDON BRIDGE

In 1790, Prince Miklos Esterhazy died, the new prince disbanded the court orchestra, and at that very moment an
impressario from England arrived, dangling a contract offer that Haydn couldn't refuse: a trip to London, more
than a dozen commissions, performance and publication
fees amounting to more than twelve hundred pounds ster-
ling, and no room on the boat for Mrs. Haydn. "How can
you do it?" asked a worried Mozart. "You speak too few
languages to go out into the world." "My language is un-
derstood everywhere," said Papa Haydn, and packed his
bags.

LONDON PRIDE

He was right. From the moment he arrived, princes, am-
bassadors, and artists waited to call upon him. He was
wined and dined, taken to parties, balls, and dances.
Crowds had to be turned away from his concerts, and
listeners in the halls cheered so loudly that whole symphony movements had to be repeated. Oxford made him
an honorary doctor, and Haydn responded by presenting

---

[16] Mozart always did like oddball challenges. He once wrote a waltz
made up of 176 separate measures that could be combined in any
order at all, depending upon throws of the dice.

the university with a tiny little piece that sounds proper whether you read it forward, backward, or upside down.[17] He became so fascinated by London that he filled up three or four notebooks with all sorts of weird information. "The Lord Mayor requires no knife at table," he wrote, "because a carver, who stands in front of him, cuts up everything in advance." "The city consumes eight hundred thousand cartloads of coal each year, each cart holding thirteen sacks." "In January, 1792, a roasting chicken cost seven shillings." [18] "The Duke of Cumberland had to pay twenty-five thousand pounds in an adultery case." When he wasn't jotting down facts and figures, Haydn was making little notes to himself so he shouldn't forget the important things he learned in England, like "the anecdote about the foot under the Duchess of Devonshire's petticoat."

LONDON DISTRACTIONS

Haydn was especially partial to the London ladies. "The sweet little thing hummed all my pieces," he marveled about the Duchess of York, going on to describe the Princess of Prussia as "the most delightful woman in the whole world." He thought Miss Brown of Bath "a most charming person," a pianist named Mrs. Hodges "the loveliest woman I ever saw," and referred to a certain Mistress Shaw

---

[17] Haydn didn't know enough English to make a speech, so at the ceremony he just took off his scholar's gown and waved it in the air.

[18] An even better bargain was "a duck, if plucked" at only five shillings.

as "the most beautiful woman I ever saw." [19] But far and away his favorite was Mrs. Schroeter, a widow who originally came to him for piano lessons,[20] but wound up staying for supper a lot. Eventually, she wrote Haydn dozens of love letters, many of which he carefully copied down in his notebooks. When he returned to London for a second visit, Haydn decided to save postage by choosing lodgings a couple of blocks away from Mrs. Schroeter's house. Meanwhile, he gave a few lessons on the side to a banker's daughter named Brassey,[21] and he also spent a lot of time with the wife of a famous surgeon, setting some of her love poems to music. After a while, the surgeon was about to return the favor by operating on Haydn's nose, but, as the composer noted, "I shouted, screamed, pounded, and kicked until I was able to free myself and hurried out of the house."

FINAL TRIUMPHS

The longer Haydn stayed in London, the more his fame and popularity grew. All of his new compositions were greeted rapturously by press and public, he was treated to fancy dinners, taken for long vacations in the country, and fussed over by the best musicians in England.[22]

---

[19] He also noted that the Prince of Wales was "the handsomest man on earth." Hmmm.

[20] Here we go again.

[21] She lived near Hertingfordbury in Hertfordshire.

[22] All except one jealous violinist-composer named Giardini who caused a bit of a scandal by calling out, at the top of his lungs, "I don't want to meet the German dog." Haydn just laughed and

Although Haydn would probably have preferred to stay home and share a nice bowl of pea soup with Mrs. Schroeter, he found himself constantly hobnobbing with royalty. He played for the Dukes of Cumberland, Clarence, Gloucester, and York; he banqueted with Baron Sir Charles Rich and at least two different lord mayors of London; he gave twenty-six command performances at parties thrown by the Prince of Wales.[23] A few months before he left for home, he was introduced to the King and Queen of England. King George had been reluctant to meet Haydn at first because he was a Handel fan and admitted that he couldn't understand "all that modern music." Queen Charlotte, on the other hand, made Haydn sing for her, invited him to all her concerts at court, and even asked him to move into Windsor Castle over the summer so they could make music together without all those other people hanging around.[24]

FAREWELL SYMPHONIES

Years earlier, at Esterhaz, Haydn had written a "Farewell" Symphony. It happened when the prince delayed return-

---

went to one of Giardini's concerts anyway. "He played like a pig," he wrote in his notebook afterward.

[23] At one of them, Haydn snitched the prince's recipe for punch, and carefully copied it in his notebook. Try it sometime, it calls for one bottle of champagne, one bottle of burgundy, one bottle of rum, ten lemons, two oranges and a pound and a half of sugar.

[24] Haydn said thank you but he had a previous engagement. When he got back to Vienna he sent a bill to the royal family for all the concerts he had played for them. It actually took a special act of Parliament, but Haydn finally got his one hundred guineas.

ing to Vienna at the end of the summer and the musicians were getting increasingly restless. They weren't allowed to bring their wives to Esterhaz,[25] and they didn't have nice fireplaces in their rooms as the prince did, so they begged Haydn to intervene on their behalf. Since he was also freezing,[26] Haydn decided to stage one of his famous musical jokes. He introduced a new symphony to the prince, with a most unusual finale. Near the end of the last movement as the players finished their parts, one-by-one they snuffed out the candles on their stands, scooped up the music parts, and tiptoed quietly off the stage. Soon most of the strings were gone with the winds, until at last only Haydn and one other violinist remained, plaintively fiddling in the gloom. His Serene Highness got the point, fortunately, and within a very few days he moved—bag, baggage, and orchestra men—back to Vienna. This time it was Haydn, himself, who was getting a bit homesick and wanted to return to Vienna, but now he was leaving behind him a dozen of his greatest symphonies, a glorious reminder of his love for London and her people. Nor did he leave empty-handed. His English friends loaded him down with presents, including six pairs of stockings with themes from his various compositions woven into the cotton, and a green parrot with a yellow tail that said "Come Papa Haydn." One of the very last pieces that Haydn wrote in England was a little song based on a folk rhyme

---

[25] A bonus as far as Haydn was concerned.

[26] "Just when I was happily dreaming of Mozart's *Marriage of Figaro*," he wrote to Marianna, "that horrible north wind woke me up and almost blew my nightcap right off my head!"

he had copied in his notebook. Since his London impressario was named Salomon, and his favorite tenor was David,
the verses must have seemed particularly apt:

King Solomon and David
led merry, merry lives.
With many, many lady friends,
and many, many wives.
But when old age came creeping on,
with many, many qualms,
King Solomon wrote the proverbs,
and King David wrote the psalms.

FINALE

Now at the age of sixty-three, Haydn was beginning to
feel a little creaky, so when he got back to Vienna he decided to give up symphonies and he never wrote another
one. In fact, he just sat there and didn't compose anything
except two famous oratorios, a couple of dozen quartets,
six or seven masses, three hundred sixty-five songs, and
the Austrian National Anthem. In his last years Haydn
was revered by everyone, with many great composers making regular pilgrimages to his doorstep.[27] No wonder that
the report of his death, in 1805, threw the entire musical
world into mourning. A London newspaper printed the

---

[27] Even when he wasn't expecting visitors, Haydn would be dressed
in his powdered wig, wearing a white neckband, a richly embroidered waistcoat of heavy silk, a dress coat of fine coffee-
colored cloth with embroidered cuffs, black silk breeches, white
silk stockings, and shoes with large silver buckles curved over the
insteps. After all, you never know when somebody's going to ring
the doorbell.

story first, and from there the news was flashed to Paris and other cities all around Europe. Letters of condolence poured in, flowers and wreaths were delivered. Kreutzer composed a violin concerto "in memory of Haydn," Cherubini published a "Cantata on the Death of Joseph Haydn," and they scheduled Mozart's Requiem at a memorial concert in Paris. Just about the only person who stayed calm and took the whole affair with his customary good humor, was Papa Haydn, himself. The reports had been completely false, of course, as he pointed out when he signed an open letter to prove that he "was still of this base world." "How can I die now?" he asked. "I have only just begun to understand the wind instruments." And when he heard about the plan for Mozart's Requiem, he said "I'm only sorry I didn't know about it on time—I would have gone to Paris and conducted it myself!"

CODA

That was Papa Haydn, father of the symphony, the string quartet, and probably the piano sonata, too. When he got around to compiling a catalogue of his compositions "as nearly as I can remember," he listed more than 100 symphonies, 83 quartets, 44 piano sonatas, 19 operas, 24 trios, 165 pieces for baryton,[28] 115 masses, 24 concertos

---

[28] Not the singing type. This baryton was a funny-looking instrument with twenty strings. Normally, Haydn wouldn't have touched it with a ten-foot bow, but Prince Esterhazy played it, and insisted that his Kapellmeister produce one baryton trio after another. The only requirement was that all the hard parts had to go to the other two players.

and literally hundreds of other pieces. The list itself was 123 pages long. But most of all, we remember Haydn for his sparkling humor, his ability to make us laugh even while we wonder at his incredibly beautiful music. "Since God has given me a cheerful heart," he said, "He will forgive me for serving Him cheerfully."

Chapter Four
A CLUTCH OF CONDUCTORS

The conductor is a peculiar person. He turns his back on his friends in the audience, shakes a stick at his players in the orchestra, and then wonders why nobody loves him. He makes the most noise at rehearsals, but there's not a peep out of him during the concerts,[1] and he only shakes hands with the musicians when everybody's ready to go home. I really don't know why people make so much fuss over conductors. I've been doing a lot of conducting lately myself, and it's very easy. You move your hands up, down, and sideways, and the music comes out.

YOUR TIME IS MY TIME
The history of conducting goes back at least as far as the ancient Greeks, who used to have somebody keep time by stomping with a special kind of boot on a stool. In the thirteenth century, one of the singers in the chorus would keep time by tapping his hand on the music book, and by the fifteenth century it became the custom for somebody

---

[1] At least there isn't supposed to be.

to beat time with a rolled-up sheet of parchment called a sol-fa.[2] By the sixteenth century, the lead singer was elected to make motions in the air "according to the nature of the marks which directs a song according to measure."[3] In most early conducting the leader would stamp his feet, clap his hands, bang a scroll on a desk, or rap the music stand with a piece of wood. The French composer Lully directed his operas by pounding out the rhythm on the floor with a heavy walking stick. One day he pounded his foot instead of the floor; that was the end of *that* method.[4] Conductors found other ways to be obnoxious, though. At the Paris Opera, the leader would place a table at the front of the stage and thump on it with a big stick "so loud," as one writer complained in 1709, "that he made a greater noise than the whole band together." Eventually they put the fellow backstage, where at least he was hidden from the audience.

PEACE AND QUIET

Gradually it dawned on people that a conductor should be seen and not heard, and sometimes his duties were taken over by members of the orchestra, usually the harpsichordist or the first violinist. One of the first great violinist-conductors was Christian Cannabich, who helped

---

[2] A pretty good name for that kind of thing.

[3] The quote comes from a book called *Musicae Activae Micrologus,* by Ornithoparcus, if my memory serves me correctlicus.

[4] It was also the end of Lully, but that's a story from my first book. (Another advertisement.)

the Mannheim Orchestra in the world's first virtuoso ensemble. As the well-known eighteenth century poet and critic Christian Schubart put it, "here the *forte* is a thunder, the *piano* a breeze of spring, the *crescendo* a cataract, the *diminuendo* a crystal streamlet babbling away into the far distance." [5]

UNCUSTOMARY CUSTOMS

There were many other ways in which concerts were different in those days. For instance, the musicians often had to stand up during performances (they did so as late as 1842, at the first concert by the New York Philharmonic), and the conductor frequently faced the audience instead of the orchestra, or else stood at one side of the stage looking toward the center. Then there was the matter of dress. When François Gossec founded the Olympia Concerts in 1770, he made his musicians wear brocade coats with lace ruffles, and plumed hats over their periwigs.[7] Perhaps the most dramatic difference, though, was to be found in the audience. In the loges, music was often considered a mere backdrop to champagne parties, poker games, and romantic encounters. Also, as Haydn noted in astonishment when he first visited London, "the common people in the galleries set the fashion with their unrestrained impetuos-

---

[5] We don't have critics like that any more.[6]

[6] Incidentally, Rosina the daughter and Carl, the son of Cannabich, turned into fine musicians, too.

[7] After some grumbling from the players, he allowed them to remove their swords during performances.

ity." If they liked something, they would yell and scream and whistle until it was encored. If they didn't, they would yell and scream and whistle until the performers fled in terror. In 1775, a Drury Lane audience hated a visiting ballet troupe so much that they ripped out the seats and hurled them onto the stage, smashed windows, defaced walls, and in general did so much damage that they had to close down the place for three months for repairs.[8]

STICK IT

You also wouldn't have recognized the early batons. Spontini used a thick ebony cane, much like a marshall's baton, with an ivory knob on either end; Berlioz worked with a heavy oak staff; Bernhard Weber preferred a roll of leather stuffed with calf's hair; Mendelssohn often settled for a rolled-up sheet of paper; and Gluck conducted with a violin bow.[9] It was Ludwig Spohr who popularized the kind of small stick we know today, because he liked to carry it in his pocket. Even so, it took quite a while for conductors to get used to it. Robert Schumann kept dropping his, until he invented a way of

---

[8] Today those riots are still fashionable—and we don't even need the dancers!

[9] Gluck once crept through the orchestra on all fours to sneak up on a dozing double-bass player and pinched him so hard the poor guy knocked over the instrument with a crash. They say Gluck was so mean that the only way he could get musicians to play in his orchestras was to bribe them with double wages.

attaching the baton to his wrist with string. At least he did better than Daniel Türk, who used his baton with such wild abandon that at one concert in England he smashed the chandelier over his head and showered the orchestra with broken glass.

BIG SHOTS

It was in the middle of the nineteenth century that the forerunners of today's superstar conductors came along, and it would take a separate volume to tell you about all of them. There was Philippe Musard, who smashed chairs and threw his baton at the players when he wasn't satisfied, and Karl Reissiger, who would look at his watch during a concert and rush the tempos if he thought his dinner might be getting cold. How about François-Antoine Habaneck, who almost wrecked the premiere of Berlioz' Requiem by reaching for his snuffbox instead of cuing in the four brass choirs, and Hans von Bulow, who conducted everything in white gloves except the Funeral March from Beethoven's *Eroica* Symphony.[10] When composers tried to conduct their own pieces, things really got out of hand. Antonin Dvořák dozed off on the podium, right in the middle of his *Stabat Mater,* until the first violinist poked him with his bow. Tchaikovsky once conducted a whole concert holding onto his head with one hand because he became convinced that otherwise it would fall off his neck; and Richard Strauss, listening to

---

[10] You guessed it. For that one movement only, he would switch to black.

the soprano at a rehearsal of his opera *Elektra,* suddenly shouted to the orchestra "Louder, louder, I can still hear her!" [11]

BARNUM'S BOY
The greatest musical showman of all was Louis Antoine Jullien, whose father had been a bandmaster in the little French village of Sisteron.[12] Jullien liked to conduct on a platform covered with crimson cloth edged in gold, using a gilt music stand and a silver baton nearly two feet long.[13] Sometimes he would draw a piccolo out of his pocket and play variations on it, and in between numbers he would wipe his brow with a silken handerchief, before sinking to rest into a huge carved armchair decorated in tapestried velvet. He also would cart in all sorts of odd instruments to supplement the orchestra, like the bom-

---

[11] "Put your left thumb in your waistcoat," Strauss advised young conductors, "and just follow the orchestra with your right. It is the audience who should sweat, not the conductor."

[12] Unfortunately, all the players in the band insisted on being the boy's godfathers, so his full name was Louis Georges Maurice Adolphe Roch Albert Abel Antonio Alexandre Noé Jean Lucien Daniel Eugène Joseph-le-Brun Joseph-Barême Thomas Antoine Pierre Carbon Pierre-Maurel Barthèlemi Artud Alphonse Bertrand Dieudonné Emanuel Josué Vincent Luc Michel Jules-de-la-Plane Jules-Bazin Julio-Cesar Jullien. By the time they'd called him for lunch it was almost dinner time.

[13] Except when he was ready to conduct something by Beethoven. Then, a liveried footman came out onto the stage to bring him a diamond-studded baton and a pair of fresh white gloves. On a silver tray, of course.

bardon, the clarichord and the octobass, which stood some fifteen feet high. Once he rattled a tin box full of dried peas to help out the tympani in the storm scene from Beethoven's *Pastoral* Symphony, and for one of his own compositions, he imitated the roar of artillery by dragging a garden roller across sheets of iron. Pretty soon P.T. Barnum heard about all this, and the circus showman brought Jullien to America for a series of spectacular concerts. One of them attracted more than forty thousand people to New York's Crystal Palace, where they were treated to Jullien's *Fireman's Quadrille,* complete with clanging firebells, full orchestra, two brass bands, and three companies of firemen in full uniform who rushed into the hall dragging their hoses behind them. Poor Barnum had to send ushers all around to assure the audience that the fire was fake and the hubbub just part of the show. They don't make conductors like that any more.

UP TO DATE
Even if we haven't produced any wild and woolly conductors in the twentieth century to equal Jullien, there have been plenty of characters all the same. To name just two, Sir Thomas Beecham got himself involved with no less than forty-seven separate lawsuits, and Artur Rodzinski used to conduct concerts with a loaded revolver in his back pocket.[14] Some of you may remember Wilhelm

---

[14] Oscar Levant said it was just his way of avoiding backtalk from the orchestra.

Furtwängler, a German conductor who used a kind of trembling motion with the baton. When he was making his debut at La Scala, the concertmaster looked at him with great pity and whispered "Courage, Maestro." Fritz Reiner had such a tiny beat that some players had trouble seeing it. During a rehearsal at the San Francisco Opera, the bass clarinetist let his head nod forward. Reiner, thinking the fellow had dozed off, stopped the orchestra and called out "Mr. Fragali, do you know where we are?" "No, I'm sorry, Maestro," the answer came back, "I'm lost, too." One of my two favorite Toscanini stories concerns one of his celebrated tantrums. The conductor had worn himself out screaming at the orchestra men, then he suddenly calmed down and said to them quietly "After I die, I shall return to earth as the doorkeeper of a bordello, and I won't let a single one of you in." The other took place in an opera house where a couple of Toscanini fans watched a performance of *Tosca* from the first row in the orchestra right behind the maestro. Surprised to see Toscanini using the music score in front of him (he often conducted opera from memory), they asked one of the musicians during intermission if the great man was beginning to get feeble. "Oh no," answered the musician, "the maestro is just running through *Tannhauser* for tomorrow night."

THE BEARDED BARONET
And finally, we come back to Sir Thomas Beecham, Bart., who used to get so carried away at his concerts that he

sometimes fell off the podium.[15] Beecham was as famous for his barbed wit as his conducting. When somebody recommended a particular soloist to him, Sir Thomas said "as a violinist he has only one defect—he can't play the violin." On another occasion, Sir Malcolm Sargent was speaking at a musical dinner in London, and mentioned that there had been a shooting incident while he was conducting a program in Israel. "Imagine that," smiled Sir Thomas, "I hadn't realized that the Arabs were so musical." Beecham was against having women in his orchestras,[16] and he didn't have much use for maestros from other countries, either. "Why do we have to have all these third-rate foreign conductors around," he grumbled, "when we have so many second-rate ones of our own?" To a not-so-efficient orchestral player Sir Thomas rumbled: "We do not expect you to follow us all the time, but do have the goodness to keep in touch with us occasionally." To a soprano: "Your voice sounds like a cart rolling downhill with the brakes on." [17] To a trombonist:

---

[15] Recently Sir Georg Solti got so excited during an opera performance that he stabbed himself in the hand with the baton and, bleeding profusely, had to leave the podium. To the credit of the musicians and singers, the opera continued flawlessly until the end of the act.

[16] "A pretty one will distract the other musicians," he explained, "and an ugly one will distract me."

[17] When she objected, "Sir Thomas, I'll have you know that I am the prima donna," Beecham was all politeness again. "Madam," he replied with a bow, "your secret is safe with me."

"Are you producing as much sound as possible from that antique drainage system you are applying to your face?" To a horse in *Aida* that had just forgotten its manners: "My God, what a critic!" And for all I know it was also Sir Thomas Beecham, Bart., who kept asking the timpanist for greater volume in the climactic part of Tchaikovsky's *Romeo and Juliet*. "A little more, please," he demanded, again and again, until the timpanist finally let go with everything he had and his mallet went right through the drumhead with a terrible ripping noise. The conductor looked up without batting an eye. "A little less, please," he said.

My father told me of a guest conductor who, during a rehearsal of *Lohengrin* at the Royal Opera in Copenhagen, repeatedly corrected the percussionist for not hitting the big drum precisely at a certain spot in the second act. The conductor told the musician to watch him carefully at that particular place in the opera and when the time came to hit the drum, he, the conductor would look at him and say "NOW!" A trifle before that point during the performance the conductor looked warningly at the percussionist, and then said—unfortunately he had a speech impediment—"Ne . . ne . . ne . . NOW it's too late."

THE WAVE OF THE FUTURE

What lies ahead? Lately more and more ensembles have been trying to get along without a conductor altogether, and some of them have been doing a pretty good job of it.[18] But I think the maestros are here to stay. They're too much fun, and life would be much too dull without what Laurence McKinney called:

This backward man, this view obstructor
Who's known to us as The Conductor.

---

[18] The first such attempt in modern times came in Moscow in 1922, and the new Soviet government loved it. "The principle of performance based on collective creative activity is a revolutionary step in music," said the chairman of the Council of Peoples Commissars. "It has reaffirmed the power of collectivism as a guiding principle in the revolutionary transformation of the social and economic system." I forget what the chairman said when the organization disbanded a few years later because the musicians found that it took too long to rehearse without a leader.

Chapter Five
FRANZ SCHUBERT

Schubert was the original bad-luck Charlie.[1] He was short, dumpy, shy, awkward, near-sighted, and his friends called him Schwammerl.[2] He wrote nine symphonies and never got to hear a single one of them played by professionals. He wrote nineteen string quartets, and eighteen of them remained unpublished at his death. He composed ten or more operas, and couldn't once come up with a decent libretto. When he tried to land a job, somebody always got there ahead of him, and the one woman he loved ran off with a bread-baker before he could scrape together enough dough to marry her himself. How fortunate he didn't discourage easily.[3]

CHEAPER BY THE DOZEN
Franz Peter Schubert was born on January 31, 1797, the twelfth of fourteen children, so who had time to notice?

---

[1] Or Franz Peter, actually.

[2] Which means Tubby.

[3] Most homes of famous composers are turned into shrines, landmarks, or museums. The house where Franz grew up is now the Schubert Garage, specializing in Volkswagen repairs.

His father, a schoolmaster, had five more when he re-married. As a small boy, Franz already showed an incredible gift for music, learning a number of instruments, and he quickly became more fluent at composing than his teachers. By the age of ten he was playing the viola in family quartets, and correcting his father whenever the old man made mistakes on the cello. This may not have been the smartest thing to do because Papa Schubert soon decided that his son shouldn't waste so much time on music after all. He took away his son's note paper, complained about his academic grades, got into some roaring arguments with the boy and eventually, when Franz was fourteen, booted him out of the house.[4]

SCHOOL DAYS

In 1808, Franz became a boy soprano in Vienna's Imperial Chapel Choir, and went to school next door at the aptly named State Konvict. Discipline was hard at the Konvict, the rooms were cold, the food scarce and, as Franz pointed out in a letter to his brother, "susceptible to improvement." [5] Still, Schubert made many loyal friends, he played violin in the student orchestra, he tried his hand at conducting, and most important of all, he was able to hear what some of his early symphonic pieces sounded like. Later he was appointed school librarian, which gave him the honor of distributing the scores, re-

---

[4] One of Schubert's first songs was called "The Father-Murderer," but he was probably just kidding.

[5] The director of the Konvict was named Innocenz, but that didn't improve the quality of the food.

placing snapped fiddle strings, oiling the oboes, and lighting the tallow candles.

SCHOOL NIGHTS

When he was seventeen, Schubert quit studying, went home, and meekly followed his father into the schoolteaching business. But his heart just wasn't in it. For three years, without slowing down his composing work, he tried to cram reading, writing, and arithmetic into the heads of squalling seven-year olds. Frequently he would run little races with himself to see how much of a new piece he could finish before the next juvenile interruption. "The little devils angered me so much that I kept losing the thread," he grumbled. "Naturally, I beat them well." Nonetheless, the list of his creations during this period is absolutely astounding: six operas, four symphonies, a couple of masses, a string quartet, several sonatas, and well over three hundred and fifty songs. Finally, in 1816, Schubert couldn't take it any more. He said a last farewell to his classes, threw in the academic towel, and went out into his native Vienna as a full-time composer. "I think I have come into the world for no purpose other than to write music," he told a friend. He was probably right.

SPEEDY LIEDER

These days we would call Schubert a workaholic. Dozens of stories are told about the unbelievable rapidity with which he turned out one extraordinary masterpiece after another. Sitting in a cafe, he won a bet that he could write an Italian-style overture within ten minutes. He dashed off the exquisite "Hark, Hark the Lark" on the back of a menu amidst the hubbub of a beer garden. He composed "The Erl King" while two of his friends stood before his writing table, watching him scribble down the notes "in no time at all." Often Schubert would chain-compose, starting another song as soon as he finished the previous one, completing seven or eight in a single day.⁶ Once he got the idea for a theme from the hum of his coffee grinder, and he completed another song while his portrait was being sketched since it was the only way the artist could keep Schubert from pacing up and down the room.

FISH STORY, CONTINUED

The next summer, Schubert went on a walking tour of Austria with the baritone Johann Vogl, and when they reached the village of Steyr they were welcomed by a local patron of the arts, Sylvester Paumgartner. He was a mine-manager by day, but his nights were filled with music, as fellow aficionados gathered in his home for regular soirees of song and sonata. Vogl must have sung "Die Forelle" at one of those sessions, because Paumgartner became captivated by the glistening tune and begged Schubert to use it in a chamber piece he could play on the cello with his friends. Within a few days, the glorious "Trout" Quintet was finished, at least all except the piano part, which Schubert improvised when they tried out the score a few nights later. The piece marked an historic first, by the

---

⁶ Sometimes he would go to bed with his glasses on so that he could continue composing as soon as he woke up the next morning.

way; no composer—not Haydn, not Mozart, not Beethoven—had ever before written a quintet for piano and
strings. Schubert was now all of twenty-two.[7]

DETOUR

Would Schubert have made a better living had he continued to concentrate on songs and chamber music? We'll
never know, of course, but it's clear that he wasted an
enormous amount of time, energy, and money trying to
become a great composer of operas. Possibly he could
even have attained that goal, but he had a positive genius
for picking inferior librettos. His first one was called *Das
Teufels Lustschloss,* which gives you an idea already. Un-
daunted by the fact that nobody would produce it, Schubert wrote four more operas by the end of that same year,
and another seven or eight later on. Nobody would produce them, either.[8]

---

[7] Do we have time to add a true trout story, even though it has
nothing to do with Schubert? In June, 1957, President Eisen-
hower attended a dairy festival in Vermont, and stayed for three
days in the town of Rutland. He loved to fish, so nearby Furnace
Brook was stocked with thousands of fresh trout from the local
hatchery. Unfortunately though, the hatchery trout had been so
well fed that they had no appetite left, and the frustrated President didn't get a single bite the whole time he was there. It was
only after he returned to Washington that the trout got hungry
again. Then the clever Vermont natives came down to the brook
and got in the best fishing of their lives.

[8] Schubert left the manuscript of one of these operas with a friend,
but it all went up in smoke because the servants used Acts Two
and Three to light the fireplaces.

The only Schubert opera that actually made it to the stage was a one-acter called *Die Zwillingsbrüder,* and better it should have stayed home. The plot was so stupid that the audience hissed it, the critics panned it, and the whole thing was withdrawn forever after six performances.

INCIDENTAL INTELLIGENCE

When Schubert wasn't writing operas with terrible librettos that nobody wanted to hear, he was writing incidental music for dreadful plays that nobody wanted to see. One of them was *The Magic Harp,* which one musical observer said was the story of "a lunatic young lady, a blubbering father, a spellbound son, and ten or twelve monsters, all mixed up with a bucket of tears and then stewed into a completely unintelligible dish of nonsense." After that he wrote the music for *Rosamunde, Princess of Cyprus,* a bomb by Helmine von Chezy that opened on December 20, 1823, and closed on December 21, 1823.[9]

ETCETERA

Schubert never could shake off his run of bad luck. But he had great good friends who loved him and his music, and there was always someone to lend him a bed, a piano, a bottle of wine, or just some encouragement when it was needed. He wrote glorious symphonies and the orchestra men said they were too hard to play. He sent some of his best songs to Goethe and the celebrated poet didn't

---

[9] At least it ran two nights. That's twice as long as *The Magic Harp.* Incidentally, Eduard Bauernfeld, another playwright of the period, described von Chezy as "a little ridiculous, and not particularly distinguished for her cleanliness."

bother to open the envelope. When he submitted "The Erl King," one of his most masterful compositions, to the publishing house of Breitkopf and Härtel, the firm not only rejected the song, but mailed it back to the wrong composer, a double-bass player in Dresden named Franz Anton Schubert.[10] Other publishers ignored or cheated him. He couldn't get anybody to perform his piano sonatas, but a local hotel swiped some of his waltzes to run in the cylinders of its musical clock. His friends misplaced his manuscripts; he himself forgot to finish some of his own best compositions. The disappointments continued all through his short life. The one and only public concert of his music took place on March 26, 1828, but the critics didn't show up. Paganini was in town, and his exploits took up all the available newspaper space. Then, later that year, just when things were finally beginning to look up—the well-known publishing house of Schott had sent him a letter inquiring about new music, and addressed to "Franz Schubert, Esq., Famous Composer in Vienna"—he suddenly took ill and passed away on November 19. He was thirty-one years old. "He has died in his greatness," said one of his friends.

BETTER LATE

Only gradually did the music lovers of the world come to realize that one of the most eloquent creative talents of all time had quietly been walking among them. He never

---

[10] "I shall retain it in my possession," Franz Anton stated, in a complaining letter to Breitkopf, "in order to learn who sent you that sort of rubbish, and to learn the identity of the scoundrel who has thus misused my name."

wanted fame or wealth, and his meager possessions weren't even worth enough to cover the funeral costs. The official list includes a mattress, pillow, and blanket, valued at six florins; two florins worth of shoes and boots; and "some old music" priced at ten florins (about five dollars). Who knows what priceless works of genius were in that bundle, to be casually distributed, or sold or burned or lost? It took eleven years for Robert Schumann to locate Schubert's mighty Ninth Symphony and arrange for Felix Mendelssohn to conduct its premiere. Another twenty-five years passed before the Viennese conductor Johann Herbeck found the manuscript of the "Unfinished" Symphony and led its first performance.[11] And it wasn't until two years after that, in 1867, that yet another Schubert treasure came to light when Arthur Sullivan found the "Rosamunde" music in a Vienna cupboard.[12] So, poor unlucky Franz Schubert came out on top after all. "Music is kind to its disciples," wrote H. L. Mencken. "When they bring high talents to its service, they are not forgotten. Life used Schubert harshly, but time has made up for it. He is one of the great glories of the human race."

---

[11] The score had been hidden by a former friend of Schubert's who had grown jealous of the master's growing fame, compared to his own obscurity. Herbeck wormed the music out of him by promising to perform one of his own overtures along with Schubert's immortal symphony.

[12] This was many years before he became Gilbert And. He was just plain Arthur, then.

Chapter Six
FELIX MENDELSSOHN

Like Franz Schubert, Felix Mendelssohn composed an incredible amount of wonderful music within an extremely short lifetime, but that's where the resemblance ends. Mendelssohn simply wouldn't have any part of the romantic image of the musician as somebody who has to suffer for his art, struggle vainly for recognition, and preferably starve to death in a miserable garret. Instead of being poor and neglected, he was rich and famous. He had nice parents and adoring sisters, his childhood was blissfully happy, he married a beautiful woman and had five lovely children. His music was played by the best performers in Europe, he was welcomed by royalty, admired by his fellow composers.[1] Even the critics liked his music.

KID STUFF
Mendelssohn was born on February 3, 1809, and right away he had a surplus of names.[2] Nobody pressured him

---

[1] Schumann called him "the Mozart of the nineteenth century," while Liszt said he was "Bach reborn." That's not bad for a start.

[2] The full list: it's Jacob Ludwig Felix Mendelssohn Bartholdy.

as a child, so Felix didn't manage to write his first song until he was five. After that he studied the piano, violin, and organ, learned several languages, became a fine swimmer, rider, bowler, and billiards player, painted lovely water colors, and turned into an elegant dancer. With all this activity, of course, he didn't have too much time left for composing, so by the time he was fourteen, Felix hadn't written anything except a few cantatas, three concertos, a bunch of fugues, several operettas, various pieces of chamber music, and a dozen symphonies.[8]

ALL IN THE FAMILY

Every Sunday there would be a morning musicale at the Mendelssohn house. His older sister Fanny was an excellent pianist, his younger sister Rebecca sang very nicely, brother Paul was a pretty good cellist, and all sorts of other local musicians would drift by to join in the fun. Sometimes Felix would be at the piano, too, or else he would bring out his fiddle, and frequently he would take a baton and stand on a stool so the players could see him conduct one of his new pieces. When Felix was sixteen his parents moved from Hamburg to Berlin, and in their new home there was a garden house, with a raised stage and a music room that could seat several hundred people. Now he could experiment with little plays, skits, and masquer-

---

[8] Before you start wishing your kids were like that, you should know that Felix also liked to climb around the roof at night, meowing like a tomcat. Once he startled a noblewoman neighbor by throwing a banana through her window.

ades, and when he and Fanny read Shakespeare's *A Midsummer Night's Dream* together, Felix set out to capture its elfin gaiety in a piano duet. It worked so well that he soon arranged it for orchestra and conducted it for his friends one midsummer's morning in his father's garden. "The guests rubbed their dazzled eyes to make sure that they were not transported too," wrote one of them about this Midsummer Night's Dream Overture, one of the most magical scores in all music.[4]

CAN YOU TOP THIS?

Once in a while Felix thought that it might be a good idea to add more music to the Overture, and in one of those "whiles" he actually tried to write some, but just couldn't get into the mood. Then, seventeen years after he had composed the overture, Mendelssohn got a rush order from the King of Prussia for incidental music for a new production of the comedy at the Palace Theater. Within two months he whipped up another dozen numbers, including the immortal Wedding March. Amazingly, the style of the new pieces exactly matched that of the Overture, despite the enormous time delay, and the suite as a whole remains astonishing in its ability to recreate,

---

[4] Speaking of dreams, Mendelssohn used to doze off at every opportunity, sometimes falling into such a deep sleep that it took him several moments to remember where he was when he awoke. "Whenever he saw a couch," says biographer George Marek, "he lay down and off he was."

as Fanny put it, "every one of the characters which Shakespeare produced in the immensity of his genius." [5]

GRAND TOUR

Mendelssohn loved traveling. He took walking trips up and down the Rhine Valley, he climbed Swiss mountains, he prowled the canals of Venice, and explored the museums of Paris. Unquestionably, though, his favorite place was England. He made ten separate trips to Britain and quickly became something of a national hero. The English hadn't had a really great composer living there since Handel, so they made a fuss over Felix, especially since he wrote big oratorios as Handel did, and gave organ recitals the way Handel used to do, and dedicated pieces to the royal family as Handel had. It's a wonder Mendelssohn never wrote any Water Music.[6] Water or not, Felix was a big hit with the English. When he conducted the C Minor Symphony there was so much cheering that he had to repeat one of the movements, and then walk through the orchestra shaking the hands of every single musician in the ensemble. When he played the organ at St. Pauls, in London, the huge crowd refused to leave the church until the verger finally disconnected the bellows in the middle of a fugue. He spent two solid hours at Buckingham Palace

---

[5] The King said he liked it, but . . . at the premiere, he insisted on holding a big tea party in his loge during the performance. According to Ferdinand David, the violinist, the clatter of spoons and the chatter of the royal guests caused such a disturbance that Mendelssohn was on the verge of stopping.

However, he wrote the Scotch Symphony, which is even better, or at least stronger.

with Queen Victoria and Prince Albert, Felix improvising on "Rule Brittania," Albert playing an organ chorale, and the Queen sightreading some of Mendelssohn's "Songs without Words." [7]

LONDON LOVE

Quite apart from the musical adulation he felt there, Mendelssohn was totally captivated by London itself. "It is the most complicated monster on the face of the earth," he wrote home, describing the wonderments of the thick fog, "the slender, beautiful women, the noisy street venders, the traffic in Piccadilly." [8] He went around to the coffee houses, the sausage shops, and the pubs; he indulged in his favorite dessert (rice pudding), and he basked in the fine London weather.[9] "There is no question," he wrote later from Naples, "that this smoky nest is my preferred city and will always remain so. I get quite emotional when I think about it."

SCOTCH SCOOP

Felix also went on an extended tour of Scotland, "with an ear for the lovely, fragrant countryside and a heart for the

[7] The only problem was the royal parrot, which had to be banished because, as Victoria put it, "he screams louder than I can sing." Felix had the honor of carrying it out of the room, cage and all.

[8] He was particularly impressed by the advertising signs. One of them, he said, "proclaimed the graceful achievements of trained cats."

[9] "Yesterday was a good day," he wrote. "That means I only got soaked through three times, and once or twice I actually caught a glimpse of the sun through the clouds."

bare legs of the natives." The trip took him to Glasgow and Edinburgh, along with such scenic locales as Inverness, Loch Lomond, and Perth. He marveled at the salt pillars and caves on the Isle of Staffa, in the Hebrides; he walked through historic castles, and he even managed to meet one of his literary idols, Sir Walter Scott. Needless to say, he left the country brimming over·with ideas like the Hebrides Overture and the Scotch Symphony. The only thing he couldn't abide was the music of the local bagpipers: ". . . infamous, vulgar, out-of-tune trash" he called it. Sorry about that, Highlanders! [10]

LOVE AND MARRIAGE
Although Felix Mendelssohn always had an eye for a pretty face or figure, he wasn't what you'd call the passionate type, and his love affairs (if indeed he had any before he got married) were totally discreet and remain undocumented. He spent some time with a pianist named Delphine von Schauroth, perhaps more than was absolutely necessary, and he was pretty friendly with the singer Jenny Lind, but that's all we know.[11] It was in 1836 that Felix met the Jeanrenauds in Frankfurt—an attractive widow named Julie and her nineteen-year old daughter Cécile. Felix began spending so much time at their house that the town gos-

---

[10] In one of his poems, Henry Wadsworth Longfellow describes the itinerant bagpiper who asked for one coin to start playing, but demanded ten before he would stop.

[11] The hottest love letter Felix ever received ends "I kiss your portrait every five minutes, imagining your presence . . . I love you, adore you, immensely." Unfortunately, it was from his sister.

sips started spreading romantic rumors about Felix and Julie. Mendelssohn couldn't make up his mind, so he left for a month at the seashore to think things over, then came back and announced his engagement to Cécile. They were married on March 28, 1837, and Felix seemed pretty casual about the whole thing. The diary of their honeymoon has sketches of people they met and places they saw, but the only entries that show real depth of feeling are the ones where the groom described some great dinners, including veal garnished with plums, and figs cooked in milk for dessert. They turned out to be very happy together, though, and if anything, their love deepened immeasurably in the ten years they had with each other.

HAPPY ENDING

Through all the short years of his life, Mendelssohn kept adding to his skills and accomplishments. He became one of the best conductors in Europe, one of the most renowned teachers, and an avid organizer of music festivals. He would sometimes have sharp words for his colleagues,[12] yet most often his tongue was in his cheek and when the chips were down he championed their music, giving first performances of pieces by Schubert, Chopin, Schumann, and many others. The great Bach revival started with Mendelssohn's historic performance of the *St. Matthew Passion,* which restored Bach's music to public attention and favor after it had lain neglected for more than seventy-

---

[12] He once referred to Rossini as "the great Maestro Windbag," and grumbled that Berlioz had "not a speck of talent," and said that Liszt had "many fingers but few brains."

five years.[13] Mendelssohn was one of the first pianists to play concertos from memory, and he never lost his astonishing abilities as an improvisor. At a musicale at Mendelssohn's home, Liszt went to the piano and played a set of fantastic variations on a Hungarian folksong. Then, to tease his host, Liszt went over to Mendelssohn and said that now it was his turn. Mendelssohn tried to beg off, but when Liszt insisted, he sat down at the keyboard and reproduced the whole set of variations that all had just heard, even throwing in a few comic imitations of Liszt's grandiose gestures, for good measure. To his credit, Liszt went along with the fun, and gladly admitted that nobody else, not even he himself, could have managed such a piece of brilliance.

CODA

So that was Felix Mendelssohn—hiker, chess-player, gourmet, musician—a fellow who felt equally comfortable chatting with Queen Victoria and drawing funny doodles for his kids. Snobby musicologists sometimes try to put down his music as not being profound enough, and in the 1930s the Nazis tried to erase him from history altogether by tearing down his statue and getting a suitably non-Jewish composer named Theo Knobel to write a substitute Wedding March.[14] But no one can erase history, and even with

---

[13] For all its monumental impact, the concert was conceived as a benefit for the Leipzig Sewing School for Girls.

[14] "Mendelssohn was an *ersatz* for a true German master," wrote one Nazi-approved author, in 1935. "His music can perhaps still be used as material for practicing, but never as a full-valued work of art."

a short life span of thirty-eight years, the genius of Felix Mendelssohn Bartholdy left us an unforgettable heritage of beautiful music. "Let us honor and love Mendelssohn," said Robert Schumann more than a century ago. "He is the prophet of a glorious future, his road leads to happiness." Or perhaps we should return to 1594 and sum up his life in the words of Shakespeare, from *A Midsummer Night's Dream,* which Mendelssohn so ennobled with his radiant score:

> Swift as a shadow, short as any dream,
> Brief as the lightning in the collied night,
> That, in a spleen, unfolds both heaven and earth,
> And ere a man hath power to say, "Behold!"
> The jaws of darkness do devour it up:
> So quick bright things come to confusion.

Chapter Seven
JOHANNES BRAHMS

They say that Johannes Brahms once left a party in Vienna, paused at the doorstep for a moment, and then called back into the house, "If there's anyone here I forgot to insult, please accept my humblest apologies." Yes, Brahms was sloppy, rude, and quick-tempered, but he wrote such incredibly beautiful music that nobody minded. Well, the critics minded, but who minds the critics? In Boston, for instance, the *Gazette's* reviewer wrote that Brahms' First Symphony is "a noisy, ungraceful, confusing, and unattractive example of dry pedantry," the man in the *Herald* called it "this tiresome waste of endless harmony," the *Evening Transcript* reported that "In the C Minor Symphony, every note draws blood . . . Brahms is an incomprehensible terror." When Boston's Symphony Hall was being constructed, critic Philip Hale suggested that there be at least one exit sign reading "This way out in case of Brahms."

CHILDHOOD
Brahms did not always have the great long beard we've all seen in paintings and photographs. In fact, as a child,

he was completely without it. He also had light hair, rosy cheeks, deep blue eyes, and a very high voice.[1] Johannes was born in Hamburg on May 7, 1833, and inherited his father's love for music. Papa Brahms played horn in a street band, double bass in the local theater orchestra, and was even the town bugler for a while, so little Johannes quickly learned to play a number of instruments himself.[2] By the time he was fifteen, he was already making a living with his music by playing in dance halls, arranging marches for brass band, giving piano lessons, and providing musical entertainment to prostitutes and their customers at various waterfront dives. At this point, though, Brahms was already deeply interested in composing. "My finest songs would come to me early in the morning while I was cleaning my boots," he recalled, many years later, "but only in great secrecy." His father figured there was no money to be made from musical composition, you see, so he tried to get Johannes to stop wasting his time with it. The younger Brahms persisted, of course, and even as he was turning into a really fine pianist, he also published more than one hundred pieces, mostly arrangements of popular tunes of the day—under the pseudonym of G. W. Marks.[3]

---

[1] His voice didn't change until he was twenty-four. That should be enough to make anybody rude and quick-tempered.

[2] He probably inherited his love of good food from his stepmother. She was a cook and her name was Schnack.

[3] If he thought a piece was worth a little more, he printed it under the name of Karl Würth.

HAPPY TO
MAKE YOUR
ACQUAINTANCE

After he passed his twentieth birthday, Brahms decided that it was time for him to go out into the world, to travel and meet other musicians who could help his career along. His first concert tour was an important step forward because he went as accompanist to the famous Hungarian violinist Eduard Reményi. Brahms' musical recall was so fantastic that he didn't bother to take any scores with him—he just played everything from memory—and once when they arrived at a hall where the piano was tuned too low, Brahms simply transposed the keyboard part up a half tone for every piece on the program. Reményi was impressed, and introduced Johannes to Joseph Joachim, another distinguished violinist from Hungary. Joachim, in turn, was struck by Brahms' "undreamed-of originality and power," and sent him on with a letter of recommendation to Franz Liszt at Weimar. When Brahms arrived, he was too shy to play his own compositions for Liszt, but the great piano virtuoso picked up Brahms' manuscripts and played them—brilliantly—at sight. Brahms was thrilled, naturally, and then sat down on the couch while Liszt, in a rare gesture of homage to the young man, played his own B Minor Sonata for him. It's a long sonata, and by the time Liszt had reached the quiet finale, Brahms was fast asleep.

So much for that friendship. Liszt invited the wide-awake Reményi to stay on with him, and poor Brahms had to go on his way alone. Eventually Brahms decided to forget about practicing for a while and he went on a long hike through the Rhineland area. There, without the pressure of performing, Brahms felt really happy for the first time. "I have passed a heavenly summer," he wrote to a friend, "rambling about for five weeks entirely according to my heart's desire." [4]

ROBERT AND CLARA
AND JOHANNES

It was on September 30, 1853, brandishing another letter of introduction from Joachim, that Brahms arrived in Düsseldorf and rang the bell at the house of Robert and Clara Schumann. Robert was overwhelmed. "A genius has arrived," he exclaimed, interrupting Brahms after only a few measures at the piano, and sending for Clara. "Listen to this," he said when his wife came in, "and you shall hear music such as you've never heard before." Clara took one look at the handsome young man at the keyboard and agreed wholeheartedly. She wrote in her diary about his "beautiful hands and interesting young face," commented on his "exuberant imagination, depth of feeling, and mastery of form," and added "may Heaven preserve his health." Before long, Brahms had done everything except move in. He took all his meals with the Schumanns, he played at their musical parties, and went strolling in the woods with Clara and her friends. When Clara left on a concert tour of Holland, Brahms followed and spent a weekend with

---

[4] The only problem was that Brahms' mother kept worrying about him. "Don't fall off the rocks," she said, "and for heaven's sake, don't go out in thunderstorms."

her in Rotterdam. Later, when she was performing in Hamburg, he took her home to meet his parents.[5] Brahms and Clara never married—even after Robert's death—probably because she wanted to devote her life to promoting Schumann's music and memory, and Brahms cherished his freedom too much. They wrote hundreds of letters to each other, though, and remained dear, beloved friends all the days of their lives.

BACK TO WORK

Meanwhile, thanks to Robert Schumann's enthusiastic appraisal of his music, Brahms found a publisher for his first important works, including two piano sonatas, half a dozen songs, and several other chamber and solo piano pieces. He was now firmly established in the composing business, and all he had to worry about were critics and audiences who often couldn't get the hang of his "modern" music. The great D Minor Piano Concerto, for instance, was a failure at its premiere in 1859, and all but booed off the stage at its repeat performance five days later. "At its conclusion," Brahms wrote to Joachim, "three pairs of hands were brought together in applause, very slowly, whereupon a perfect storm of hissing from all sides forbade any further such demonstration." [6] Seven years later

---

[5] With apparently no etchings to show, Brahms let Clara see his precious collection of tin soldiers.

[6] "The usefulness of this concerto," wrote one critic, "was that the pianist was permitted to show how excellent a football player he

came the glorious German Requiem,⁷ and the year after that the first of the four symphonies that would rank Brahms among the immortals of orchestral writing.⁸

SUCCESS

Despite the critics, Brahms' music was being more and more widely performed, and audiences gradually realized that there was indeed a genius in their midst. They were delighted with the bouncy rhythms of the Hungarian Dances, they thrilled to the expansive Violin Concerto, they sat entranced by the gorgeous sonatas and other chamber music. Brahms was celebrated, revered, sought after, fussed over, and he responded by producing one masterpiece after another. Oddly enough, the biggest brickbats coming his way now were from other composers possibly jealous of his triumphs. "Whoever can swallow this concerto," wrote Hugo Wolf after Brahms appeared as soloist in the premiere of his Second Piano Concerto, "will be able to get along splendidly in times of famine on the nu-

---

would make. He thrashed the piano until one feared its legs would crumble under the mighty onslaught."

⁷ "The colossally stupid Requiem," George Bernard Shaw called it, "which has made so many of us wish ourselves dead. It is so execrably and ponderously dull that the very flattest of funerals would seem like a ballet after it."

⁸ "It would appear as though Brahms might afford occasionally to put a little melody into his work—just a little, now and then, for a change," said the *Boston Traveler* about the Second Symphony. Said London's *Saturday Review* about the Fourth: "There is no more intolerably dull symphony in the world than the E Minor."

tritive equivalent of window glass, cork stoppers, and stove pipes." [9] Brahms also came to the realization that he no longer had to be polite to publishers in order to get his music printed, or butter up conductors to get his symphonies played. He could just sit back and do what he pleased and if somebody didn't like it, too bad for them. So he quit doing things he didn't want to do—like practicing the piano—and he continued doing things he did want to do—like conducting women's choruses [10] and growing his famous beard.

BUSHY TALE

Just why Brahms decided to sprout a luxurious beard remains something of a mystery. Some say it was so that he wouldn't have to wear a necktie any more. Others think Brahms just wanted to appear more mature. "Before I had my beard," he said, "I looked like Clara Schumann's son; now with it, I look like her father." "With a shaven chin," he pointed out to another friend, "people take you either for an actor or a priest." In any event, a new era arrived for the bearded Brahms—one where he was going to be comfortable—and never mind what polite society

---

[9] Tchaikovsky was much more tactful. "I played over the music of that scoundrel Brahms," he entered in his diary for October 9, 1886. "What a giftless bastard!"

[10] "Their clear, silver tones please me exceedingly," he said, "and in the church, with the organ, the ladies sound quite charming." Brahms' favorite pupil in the choir, by the way, was named "Friedchen." "She can do all kinds of things with her little fingers," he explained.

thought about it. He had always tended to be a bit on the sloppy side anyway; [11] at this point, he really indulged himself. He walked around Vienna in an old brown coat smudged with cigar ashes, his felt hat was so badly battered that he usually carried it around in his hand instead of putting it on his head, and in bad weather he wrapped himself up in a tattered, odd-looking shawl, held together in front by an enormous safety pin.[12] One day while Brahms was out somebody came to visit him. The door was unlocked so the fellow entered and looked around the room and was shocked to see papers strewn all over the floor, and a thick layer of dust covering the piano. Disgustedly, he traced the word "Pig" in the dust, and left. A few days later, he met the composer on the street and mentioned the incident. "I know," Brahms snorted, "I found your calling card!"

BARKS AND BITES

Since there seemed to be no further need to watch his tongue either, Brahms proceeded to best many a musician in verbal battles of wit. When a Viennese composer came to him after a premiere and said "A splendid work, your new symphony, only sometimes it reminds me of some other music," Brahms snapped back "What other music— your next symphony?" When a singer kept rejecting his pieces because they were too well-known, Brahms sug-

---

[11] When he was a young man, Brahms used to mend rips in his trousers with sealing wax.

[12] Sometimes he forgot to button his suspenders so once, during a concert, his pants started sliding down while he was conducting.

gested "take some of my posthumous songs. Nobody will know them at all." And when Brahms was trying out his new sonata with a not-so-good cellist, he played the piano part louder and louder until the cellist called out "Please I can't hear myself at all." "You're lucky," said Brahms, hitting another fortissimo, "I still can!" Perhaps remembering what other composers had said about his music, Brahms no longer was bashful about commenting on theirs. After seeing Anton Rubinstein's opera *Nero,* for example, he agreed that "the music is a most appropriate description of the Emperor's character—it's horrible!" And when someone praised a new piece by the young Richard Strauss, Brahms replied simply, "If it's Strauss I much prefer Johann, and if it's to be Richard, I'd rather have Wagner." On the other hand, he could also turn his humor against himself. Once when he was invited to lunch by an eminent wine merchant, a rare old bottle of Rauenthaler was opened at the end of the meal. "What Brahms is among composers," the host exclaimed proudly, ".this Rauenthaler is among wines." "Well then," Brahms called out, "how about opening a bottle of Bach?" [18]

FINALE

So, Brahms spent his last years happily, composing, walking in the mountains, drinking good German beer, and

---

[18] Occasionally Brahms did come out on the short end of the satiric stick. Once walking with his friend, the singer and conductor George Henschel, they passed a building with a commemorative plaque on it. "The day after I die they'll put up a sign on my house, too," said Brahms. "Of course they will," Henschel agreed. "It'll say 'House to Rent.' "

flirting with many women, although he never married any of them.[14] He came pretty close to proposing to Agathe von Siebold but then changed his mind at the last moment. "I love you," he wrote her, "I want to come again to clasp you in my arms and to kiss you, but you must understand that I am incapable of being fettered." That wasn't enough for Agathe, so she married somebody else, and Brahms settled for weaving her name into a sextet. He wasn't lonely, though. He had a lively relationship with a pretty young singer named Hermine Spies, developed a crush on Clara Schumann's daughter Julie, and when he was almost sixty, he was enchanted by another singer named Alice Barbi. But he was well content to let his girl friends find husbands elsewhere, especially after he realized that he could still see them once in a while anyway.[15] Brahms' music was now universally admired, of course, and on March 7, 1897, he attended a Philharmonic concert in Vienna where his Fourth Symphony was greeted so tumultuously that he had to stand up again and again to acknowledge the roar of applause that rocked the auditorium at the end of each movement. Less than a

---

[14] "I feel about matrimony the way I feel about opera," he wrote to the critic Hanslick. "If I tried it once, I probably would do it again, but I can't seem to make up my mind to undertake either one of them for the first time."

[15] An amateur musician named Edward Speyer was married to one of Brahms' old flames, and in his memoirs, he tells of the time he went to meet the composer at the Frankfurt railway station. "I ran to the compartment which Brahms had already opened," Speyer reported, "and he flung his arms around me. Then, he suddenly shoved me back, saying 'Oh, forgive me, I thought you were your wife!' "

month later, the ships in the Hamburg harbor were flying
their flags at half-mast, and the world mourned the death
of Johannes Brahms. One of the immortals of music had
passed away, but not without having made his peace on
earth. His very last composition was a chorale prelude on
the words:

Oh world, I now must leave thee,
And go on the journey to my eternal home.
I faithfully and humbly commit my soul and body
Unto the Lord's all-loving hands.

Chapter Eight
A POUNDING OF PIANISTS

TOP OF THE LINE

I do not recall who taught me the history of the piano, but it is possible that in a dream I learned that the first piano ever built had only one big black key. Naturally, this frustrated the then contemporary composers who found it very difficult to write variations on a theme or, for that matter, any sensible music at all on a single note. It was not until someone invented the cracks that more tones became available, and with the influence of the civil rights movement, the keyboard finally appeared as we know it today.

And so we come to the piano, the most wonderful, self-sufficient, and out-of-tune instrument of them all. The organ is bigger and the harpsichord has more keyboards and the accordion is lighter and the glockenspiel is tinklier, but when seated at the piano, one may feel a whole orchestra in their hands. It's like controlling ten instrumental sections, playing the melody and counter-melodies with the accompaniment all together, and still having a finger or two left over to make mistakes with. (At the moment I am writing a piano concerto for wrong notes only; but as I progress I find that similar pieces have been done before.) You may go as high as the piccolos and as low as the tubas, play so quietly that you can hardly hear a thing, and loud enough to drown out a whole symphony òrchestra. Of course, playing the piano badly (even if it's in tune), can be more dreadful than any other instrument, so one must be benevolent.[1]

THE GRAND PIANO

Now, if the following anthology of the piano is in accordance with established facts, I must reluctantly concede to my notion that the previous description of the birth of that instrument must have been conceived in a dream.

Credit for the invention of the piano is usually given to Bartolommeo Cristofori, an Italian harpsichord maker in the service of Prince Ferdinando de' Medici.[2] Cristofori had made about forty harpsichords for the Prince, and was starting to get a little bored with the whole process, when he got a brainstorm. This was to construct an instrument where, instead of plucking the strings the hammers would strike them, harder or more softly, with exactly the same strength as they do in a harpsichord. This doesn't sound terribly revolutionary, but in 1709 it opened the ear to a whole new world of sound. Since the player could control the volume by means of touch, Cristofori

---

[1] Ambrose Bierce, the famous humorist, came away from one recital saying that the piano is operated by "depressing the keys of the machine and the spirits of the audience at the same time."

[2] In Germany, Christoph Gottlieb Schröter wrote all sorts of articles to prove that he was the one who had the idea first. He wasn't, as you already know.

called his new contraption "gravicembalo col piano e forte," which means "harpsichord with soft and loud." [3]

GROWING UP

The early pianos, needless to say, weren't anything to brag about. They had funny shapes, fewer notes, no pedals, and they were weaker, clumsier, and went out of tune more quickly than our modern instruments.[4] Considering some of the nutty people who tried to make improvements over the next hundred years, it's a wonder the piano wasn't abandoned altogether. There was Anton Häckle, who tried to stick a small organ underneath the piano keyboard to sustain the melody better, and Matthias Müller, who devised a piano with two keyboards facing each other. Carl Leopold Röllig came up with a keyboard that propelled little bows across the strings, and William Southwell invented a foot pedal that operated a page-turning attachment. In Philadelphia, Isaac Hawkins developed a folding keyboard, while somewhere else Joseph Merlin was proud of his gadget that attempted to vary the sound volume by foot pressure rather than finger touch.[5] In 1840 the Broadwood Piano Company produced a combined piano and

---

[3] When they started building the new instruments in France and Germany, they called them fortepianos instead of pianofortes. Why not leave well enough alone?

[4] Ha!

[5] Merlin also invented a mechanical tea table that simultaneously could pour out a dozen cups. Sort of a nineteenth century "Tea for Twelve."

writing desk, and even a flat piano-table from which the entire works of the piano could be removed, like a drawer.[6] Less than fifteen years later, Daniel Hewitt figured out a way of attaching the strings to the wall of his house, thus saving the expense of a piano frame. And a dozen years after that, a fellow named Millward patented "a combination piano, couch, closet, and bureau, with toilet articles." During the same period, pianos were built in the shape of an 8-foot-tall giraffe; they were covered with pearl, marble, ivory, or tortoise shell; sculptors were commissioned to chisel bronze mouldings on the instruments, and painters decorated every available surface with original oils.[7]

All this time, of course, the real geniuses of piano building were quietly developing the instrument into the marvel we know today, and founding the companies that still bear their names: Steinway, Chickering, Baldwin, Kimball, Bechstein, Blütner, Büsendorfer.[8] And with the piano itself reaching such heights of perfection, the stage was set for a different type of wild character to emerge—The Pianist.

UNLOCKING THE KEYS
The first public appearance by a pianist anywhere seems to have occurred at Covent Garden in May, 1767 when, during the intermission of *The Beggars Opera,* "Miss

---

[6] The character who added a drumstick, to pound on the piano's sounding board, at least had the decency to remain anonymous.

[7] Seems that I was still dreaming!

[8] When Ludwig Bösendorfer died, in 1919, his will specified that he be carried to the cemetery in a piano van. There's dedication for you.

Brickler sang a song accompanied by Mr. Dibdin on a new instrument called the pianoforte." [9] A year later, also in London, one of the more talented chips off the old Bach, Johann Christian, gave the world's first piano recital. The papers said he played on a *Zumpe Square Piano*.[10] It was in the nineteenth century, though, that the age of virtuosos was born, led by a dazzling array of pianists who tried to outdo each other as well as astonishing audiences with their own incredibly difficult compositions. Franz Liszt was the champion in that department (he was so famous that I'm going to save him for the next chapter), but he had lots of competition. There was Jan Ladislav Dussek, who was the first one to think of placing the piano sideways on the stage so that the ladies could admire his beautiful profile.[11]

LIGHTING UP

Another famous nineteenth century pianist-composer, Adolphe Henselt, used to get so nervous before a concert that he would hide in the wings while the orchestra played the opening section of a concerto and rush out at the very last possible moment to play his solo part. One evening he zoomed out so fast that he forgot to put away his cigar first, and he had to puff his way through the whole first movement.

---

[9] Remember, in Germany and France the instrument was called fortepiano, which really doesn't make that much difference.

[10] Well, it was a start.

[11] Dussek used to sit at the keyboard a little left of center because he thought it would make the bass notes sound louder.

A NEW WORLD
OF VIRTUOSITY

In America, audiences never knew what to expect at concerts. A pianist named Hatton liked to attach a sleigh bell to his ankle so that he could jingle an accompaniment to his playing, and sometimes he had an assistant come out on stage and play duets with him on a contraption that sounded like the cracking of a whip—a display of artistry, according to *Dwight's Journal of Music,* that would "arouse a storm of applause which had no end." Daniel Seibelt gave concerts with his wife banging a tambourine alongside the piano, and Louis Moreau Gottschalk wrote a piece for himself and thirty-eight pianists to play at the same time. Even the world-renowned European virtuosos who came to tour in this hemisphere were swayed by America's love of the unexpected. Leopold de Meyer was soon nicknamed the "Lion Pianist," not only because of his huge shock of hair, but because he liked to emphasive exciting parts of the music by smashing the keys with his fists. De Meyer also had the disconcerting habit of moving the piano around to different parts of the stage in the middle of a concert, and when he got tired of playing, he'd make speeches to the audience, instead.[12] When Henri Herz came to the United States a year later, in 1846, he an-

---

[12] Well, who doesn't? [13]

[13] At least it is better than what happened when de Meyer toured Turkey and was invited to perform at the Sultan's Palace. Unfortunately, the only piano in the place was one that was kept inside the harem, and its legs had been drastically shortened so that the Sultan's wives could play it seated on floor cushions.

nounced that the only way he could get into the proper mood for his recital was for the hall to be lighted by one thousand candles. That whetted everybody's curiosity so much that the concert was sold out within a day.[14]

RUSSIAN JEWEL

The greatest of all the nineteenth century pianists in Russia was Anton Rubinstein; the Americans quickly dubbed him "Ruby" when he arrived for a tour in 1872. Actually, Rubinstein hadn't been at all eager to visit what he thought was still a backward and uncultivated country, so he insisted on a clause in his contract specifying that he "would not be obliged to play in beer gardens or tobacco establishments." Since he was also suspicious of the value of the American dollar,[15] Rubinstein demanded payment in gold. He began to regret it when, after having given more than two hundred concerts, he was presented with a bag of coins weighing one hundred forty pounds. At least he gave audiences their money's worth. At one concert, he played eight Beethoven Sonatas, then tossed in the entire Chopin B-flat Minor Sonata as an encore. Whatever the opposite of insomnia is, Rubinstein had it. He was such a sound sleeper that only one thing would get him up in the morning. His wife would go upstairs and play an un-

---

When de Meyer complained, the Sultan had to get three slaves to hold the piano on their backs during the entire concert.

[14] After the first piece, somebody complained in a very loud voice that there were actually only 992 candles. There's always one in every crowd.

[15] So what else is new?

resolved chord on the piano.[16] Rubinstein couldn't stand it, so he would run up the stairs in his nightshirt to play the proper finishing notes. Meanwhile, Mrs. R. would take all the sheets off the bed so he couldn't get back in, and the master's day could now begin. Like so many of his colleagues, Anton Rubinstein was a better pianist than a composer, although one of his pieces, the Melody in F, became so popular in America that almost everybody had to play it. When Josef Hofmann scheduled it at one of his concerts, against his better judgment, a lady came backstage and gushed "Oh Maestro, how much you put into that piece!" "God knows I had to," Hofmann snapped back, "Rubinstein certainly didn't!"

MODERN TIMES

As we turn the corner into our own twentieth century, we find many other distinguished pianists arriving on the scene, some of them as nutty as those before them. There was Teresa Carreño, who kept marrying other musicians until people lost count,[17] and Vladimir de Pachmann, who started divorce proceeding against his fourth wife at the age of eighty-five. De Pachmann, by the way, was nick-named the "Chopinzee" because of his antics on stage. One time he refused to start a concert because the piano bench was too low. He paced up and down, grumbling loudly to the audience, until a stagehand heard the com-

---

[16] For the uninitiated: to resolve a chord is the fulfillment of an expectation. Resolved?

[17] "At yesterday's concert," reported one critic, "Frau Carreno played for the first time the second concerto of her third husband."

motion and brought out a telephone book. De Pachmann
tried it, shook his head disdainfully, then carefully tore
out one single page. The problem solved, he sat down
again, beamed happily at the audience, and began playing. At another concert, an all-Chopin recital, de Pachmann hung a pair of socks on the piano, announcing that
they had once been worn by Chopin himself.[18]

POLES OF ATTRACTION

Two of Poland's most famous musicians were also enormously popular in America. Moriz Rosenthal and Ignace
Jan Paderewski both lived into their eighties (each died
in New York in the 1940s), performing until the last.
Rosenthal was the last in the celebrated line of Franz
Liszt's pupils, but he was almost more famous for his
sharp tongue than his fleet fingers. When he was invited
to a party at the home of a Viennese composer, Rosenthal
noticed scores by Bach, Brahms, and Mozart strewn on
the piano. "My goodness," said the pianist in surprise, "I
always thought you composed by ear." Later, he over-
heard somebody asking another pianist to write something very brief in an autograph album. "Why don't you
just put down your repertoire?" he suggested. Rosenthal
used to travel with a silent keyboard so that he could
practice in hotel rooms while he was on tour. Once he
was quietly doing his scales when a maid came in and
stood watching him in puzzlement. Rosenthal looked up

---

[18] Offstage, de Pachmann was pretty odd too. He milked cows because he said it kept his fingers well exercised, and before every
concert he would dip his fingers, one by one, into a glass of
brandy. Maybe it helped with the high notes.

and explained that he was using a magic piano that could be heard only by people who had not sinned within the past twenty-four hours. As he told it later, the maid blushed furiously and rushed out of the room.[19]

As a young music student in Vienna and Berlin, I often saw and heard Moritz Rosenthal and was—like all others—awed by his piano playing. Years later, a few days after my arrival as a refugee in New York City, I passed the tall windows of the then Horn and Hardart Automat cafeteria on 57th Street and, as if in shock, waved at the distinguished gentleman seated alone at a table in view of the windows. Obviously Moritz Rosenthal didn't recognize the silly guy in the street, but he waved back anyway.

IN THIS CORNER

Just as the Americans had christened Anton Rubinstein "Ruby," they were quick to show their affection for Paderewski by dubbing him "Paddy." He made his debut at Carnegie Hall in 1891, and subsequently gave hundreds and hundreds of concerts in every part of the country. His wild unruly hair and handsome features caused a sensation everywhere almost as great as the won-

---

[19] On another occasion, though, Rosenthal got his own back. He had been rattling off one hilarious anecdote after another at a dinner party, when one of the other guests asked him to continue his recollections later in the week at another soirée. Rosenthal agreed, arrived on schedule, had a fine dinner and then, feeling in an expansive mood, went to the keyboard and favored the company with an hour of Chopin. When he finished, there was his delighted host clapping him on the back: "Why that was absolutely marvelous, Mr. Rosenthal, I had no idea you could play the piano, too!"

der at his brilliant playing. By 1896 Paderewski was such a popular figure that his local appearances were front-page news. When he played in New Orleans that year the *Daily Item* had no music critic on its staff. Since the event had to be covered, a sportswriter was assigned to the concert.[20] Before long, every budding pianist in America was playing Paderewski's Minuet in G, the Metropolitan Opera had presented his grand opera *Manru,* and the Boston Symphony Orchestra was preparing the premiere of his B Minor Symphony. Awarded honorary degrees by at least four major American universities, he established scholarships for deserving musicians and gave away millions of dollars to worthy causes of every sort. Toward the end of his career he even appeared in a Hollywood movie. I must admit that the more his fame grew, the more eccentric he became. During his final American tours, he traveled in a private railroad car he designed himself. It had comfortable chairs, his favorite books, an independent lighting and heating system and, of course, his own grand piano. His entourage consisted of his private tuner,

---

[20] "In my opinion," wrote that worthy in the next edition, "Paderewski is the best two-handed piano fighter that ever wore hair. After landing heavily with his left on the bass end of the keyboard, with a smash that rattled the chandeliers, he got in a right-hand smash or two over the heart that would put any ordinary box of wires out of business. Paddy let up a bit in the second round, which gave the piano a chance to get its second wind, but the man with the mess of hair was only saving his steam for the finale. The air in front of that piano was filled with flying hands and hair. The practiced ear might have picked out of the crash and jumble a concord of sweet sounds, but I was too busy looking to listen. If I were a piano, I wouldn't travel as Paderewski's sparring partner for two-thirds of the gross receipts."

valet, chef, secretary, physician, and masseur; and occasionally, for games of bridge in the evenings. three extra friends.[21] Paderewski had his hands insured for $100,000, and when he got tired of touring, he became Premier of Poland.[22]

At fourteen, in my hometown of Copenhagen, I saw and heard Paderewski at an unforgettable concert. The second time I only *saw* Paderewski . . . when among the thousands of mourners I passed his bier at St. Patrick's Cathedral in New York in 1941.

FINALE

I could tell you lots about other famous pianists, like the American virtuoso who once leaped off the stage to slug a fan who had dared to take a picture of him, or the Canadian who demanded that the studio technicians turn off the air conditioning at a recording session because he couldn't hear himself hum. But I must finish with a true story about one of the world's dumbest music critics. It happened in St. Louis, when Oscar Levant was soloist with the Symphony. The applause following the concerto was so extravagant that Levant finally had to come out for a solo encore. He played a short Gershwin Prelude, explaining to the audience that he couldn't do anything further because he had to catch a train. You guessed it. The next day, the critic wrote that Mr. Levant was at his best in "I've Got to Catch a Train."

---

[21] That was just for him, by the way. His wife took along her own staff.

[22] Some people will go to any lengths to avoid having to practice.

Chapter Nine
FRANZ LISZT

Since Franz Liszt was probably the greatest pianist of all time, I've set aside a whole chapter just for him. But we must begin with Prince Esterhazy. You remember my telling you about him.[1] What happened is that one of the servants in his employ was a man named Adam Liszt. Adam played the piano, violin, and guitar, although evidently not too well, because the prince sent him away from the main palace to take charge of some properties in Raiding, a little Hungarian village about thirty miles from Vienna, and therefore safely out of earshot. There wasn't much else to do in Raiding, so on October 22, 1811, Adam's wife gave birth to a baby boy. His name was Franz Liszt.[2]

SLOW START
At first, Franz didn't seem to be any great bargain, even as children go. He was sickly, nervous, weak, and he

---

[1] If not, reread the chapter on Haydn, but please stay awake this time.

[2] Actually, his name was Liszt Ferencz, because the Hungarians sign in backwards, but we'll call him Franz Liszt and that's that.

fainted a lot. He really liked music, though, and when his
father started giving him piano lessons, Franz would sit
practicing scales and exercises for hours at a time.[3]

At the age of nine he gave his first concert, and
Adam was so proud of his son that he arranged to have
him perform for Prince Esterhazy. The prince in turn
was impressed enough to invite Franz to play for other
members of the aristocracy at one of his palaces. His wife,
Princess Esterhazy, was so enchanted that she gave the
boy a valuable autograph book that he lost almost immediately, even though it had belonged to the immortal
Haydn himself.[4] At the concert, Franz not only improvised on themes called out to him by the audience, but
he sight-read some very difficult pieces that the noblemen
placed before him. They were so astonished and impressed that afterward, the counts Apponyi, Amadee,
Erdody, Szapary, and Viczay put their pocketbooks together and gave Franz six hundred gulden a year, for six
years, to help with his studies.[5] Papa Liszt was even more
thrilled than his son. With visions of his little *wunder-
kind* reaping huge fortunes for him, Adam Liszt quit his
job and took Franz to Vienna, the musical capital of
Europe.

---

[3] He worked at them so hard that he started to get weak, faint, etc.,
until papa stopped the lessons. That made Franz even more nervous, sickly, etc., so papa started them again.

[4] Easy come, easy go.

[5] In those days, an Austrian gulden was worth about 50 cents.

PRODIGY AT WORK

Liszt's first teacher in Vienna was Karl Czerny, who wrote hundreds and hundreds of compositions, but whose name will always be associated with those finger-breaking exercises that all student pianists have slaved over from his day to ours.[6] Czerny was at it then, too, standing over ten-year old Franz for three hours every day, smoking his pipe and making him repeat passages over and over again until the boy was ready to scream.[7] If Franz was getting impatient with all those finger exercises, Papa Liszt was fairly jumping out of his skin. He wanted his son to perform and be admired and earn piles of money, and not stay home all day doing "dull and uninspired" practice work. Finally he couldn't stand it any longer and organized a big concert for little Franz on April 13, 1827—the date when Liszt's career really started. Franz had been well prepared by Czerny, and he was a tremendous success, playing a Piano Concerto by Hummel and his own Fantasia based on the slow movement of Beethoven's Fifth Symphony.[8] After that, Papa Liszt took his boy on tour. He played in Munich, Stuttgart, and Strasbourg. In

------

[6] Czerny arranged the *William Tell* Overture for thirty-two hands on eight pianos.

[7] Czerny called Liszt "Putzi." I'd hate to know what Liszt called Czerny.

[8] Beethoven was in the audience that day, and since he was too deaf to hear what Liszt had done to his symphony, he came up onstage and kissed the boy on the forehead.

Paris he appeared before dukes and duchesses; in London he was welcomed by King George IV. Papa collected the money, Franz was happy when he could get a nice plate of gooseberry pie, and the Liszt legend had begun.

In 1827 Adam Liszt died suddenly, and Franz moved back to Paris dedicated to a career as pianist, teacher, and composer. He was now sixteen. "Women will bring you under their sway and give you trouble all your life," was his father's last prediction, although Liszt had no idea what he was talking about. "I didn't even know what a woman was," he wrote, many years later, "and in my simplicity I asked my priest to explain the sixth and ninth commandments to me, for I was afraid I might have broken them without knowing I had done so." A few months later, he knew. He had started giving piano lessons and he fell in love with one of his students, seventeen-year old Carolyn de Saint-Cricq. The first indication came when the lessons began getting longer and longer.[9] They were now reading mushy poems to each other, underlining romantic novels, and talking until midnight. It was all very lovely until her father caught them one night and kicked Liszt out of the house. Poor Franz was so upset that he went into hiding and moped around the house for two years, reading Byron and books on socialism. He stayed in seclusion for so long that a Paris newspaper actually printed his obituary. Fortunately, Liszt decided that women were more fun than socialism after all, so eventually he joined the rest of the world.

---

[9] And with less and less playing (piano, that is).

A TOUCH OF THE FIDDLER

On March 9, 1831, Liszt went to the first concert given in Paris by Niccolo Paganini. The famous violinist played his fantastic virtuoso pieces with everybody cheering like crazy and women were swooning left and right. Liszt was so overwhelmed by the experience that he vowed then and there to become the Paganini of the Piano. Let women throw themselves at *his* feet for a while. He studied and he read and he practiced. "My mind and my fingers are working like two lost souls," he wrote to one of his students. "I learn, I meditate, and in addition I work four or five hours every day at thirds, sixths, repeated notes, and other exercises. If only I don't go mad, you will find an artist in me." After several years of this kind of slavery, Liszt started playing in public again with women swooning left and right for him, too.[10]

A LISZT OF ROMANCES

Equally true to Paganini's image as a Don Juan, Liszt allowed his own love life to get terribly complicated. Let's see, there was a pianist named Camille, an actress named Charlotte, and a singer named Sabatier. There was the Baroness Olga and the Princess Belgiojoso. There was Marie Duplessis, the courtesan whose life became the model for *La Traviata,* and Marie Mouchanoff-Kalergis,

---

[10] Sometimes Liszt was so carried away that he himself would swoon right in the middle of a performance. According to one eyewitness, "he fainted in the arms of a friend who was turning pages for him, and we bore him out in a strong fit of hysterics."

who stood six-feet tall, and Lady Blessington, who said "What a pity to put such a handsome man at a piano." There was Robert Franz and George Sand and Daniel Stern, all of whom were women, Liszt said.[11] There was the famous dancer Lola Montez, who once followed Liszt to an all-male banquet, burst into the room and proceeded to dance a fandango on a dinner table. There was Agnes, a spy who traded her charms for information about political refugees, and Olga, a Cossack horsewoman from the Ukraine,[12] who was so jealous of Liszt that she tried to stab him with a poisoned dagger. When Liszt played at private homes, women would press around him at the piano and pull souvenir hairs out of his head with little tweezers. They would enter his hotel bedroom in his absence and carry off in bottles some of the water from his washbowl. At fancy restaurants women fought each other for the privilege of drinking the leftover tea in his cup. One American woman stripped the covering off a chair Liszt had been sitting on, framed it, and hung it on her wall. An elderly lady caused a good deal of comment because she always exuded a curious tobacco odor even though she never smoked or took snuff. Finally she confessed that, twenty-five years earlier, after a public dinner, she had stolen the stump of Liszt's cigar and had been carrying it around in her corsage ever since.

---

[11] Come to think of it, he had three children with Daniel Stern, so he wasn't completely mistaken.

[12] Her first piano teacher died when her pet tiger bit him.

MAKE MINE MARIE

The first of Liszt's major love affairs started in 1833, when he went to a party at Chopin's apartment in Paris, and met the Countess Marie Catherine Sophie d'Agoult. She was a bit older than he (twenty-eight to his twenty-two), well-educated, charming, sophisticated, beautiful and, by nineteenth century standards, a trifle forward. Right after that first meeting, she wrote Liszt a letter asking him to come up and see her some time.[13] Liszt remembered what one writer called Marie's "bewitchingly graceful movements" and the profusion of blonde hair that fell over her shoulders like a shower of gold," grabbed his hat and rushed right over. "We embarked at once upon serious conversations," wrote Marie in her diary. "We talked of the destiny of mankind, of its sadness and uncertitude, of the soul, and the future life." [14] As time went by, Marie and Franz stopped pretending that their relationship was purely platonic [15] and ran off to Geneva together. There, Marie tried to improve Liszt's mind by making him read books on religion and attend philosophy lectures, and Liszt tried to improve his eyesight by giving free piano lessons to some of the prettiest students at the university.

----

[13] She also sent a similar note to Chopin, saying that she had a cold and "one of your nocturnes would complete my cure. If you can't come tomorrow," she added, "make it Saturday. If not Saturday, Sunday." Some people have no patience at all.

[14] Sure they did.

[15] It had become more and more difficult, especially after Marie became pregnant.

He even marked down the special attributes of his pupils in a little notebook. For instance, "Julie Raffard: very small hands, but brilliant fingerwork." "Jenny Gambini: gorgeous eyes." "Marie Demallayer: lots of enthusiasm. Makes faces and contortions."

ON THE ROAD AGAIN

Marie would probably have been content to stay home indefinitely, but applause was in Liszt's blood and he quickly became itchy for the stage. This was all the more true because reports had filtered back from Paris that a pianist named Sigismond Thalberg was challenging his supremacy as the most famous virtuoso of the day.[16] So Liszt returned to the French capital, and in March, 1837, the two pianists undertook a series of musical duels, culminating in a concert where both of them performed their most difficult pieces. The verdict was not long in coming: Thalberg was an exceptionally fine artist, but Franz Liszt stood alone. Soon afterward, he embarked on an extended series of European concert tours that brought him even more smashing successes. He was cheered from Constantinople to Copenhagen, from Milan to Moscow. He performed for Queen Victoria at Buckingham Palace and at the court of Czar Nicholas I of Russia; he was welcomed by the nobility in Poland, Italy, and Austria.[17]

---

[16] I am not much for gossip, but did you know that Thalberg was the illegitimate son of Prince Moritz Dietrichsten and the Baroness von Wetzlar? Remember, you heard it here first.

[17] Actually, he had a little trouble in Austria because the empress heard of some of his adventures, and insisted that he be investigated first by her police minister. The report says that Liszt had

UPPER CLASS

Perhaps the greatest triumph of all came when Liszt returned to his native Hungary, to be greeted by military bands, torchlight processions, serenades, cheering crowds, ceremonies, dinners, dances, and the gift of a sabre inlaid with precious stones. The only bad part was that Liszt had to shell out one thousand francs for an elegant Hungarian uniform, and then say thank you in French because he had completely forgotten his childhood Hungarian. He was disappointed in one other matter, too. Cavorting with all those noble men and women around Europe made him all the more keenly aware of his own lowly birth, and he had mounted a campaign to have the Hungarians bestow a title of nobility upon him. As a matter of fact, he was just trying to decide whether to put a lyre, a harp, a roll of manuscript paper, or perhaps an owl (for wisdom) on his coat of arms, when the whole deal fell through. A disappointed Liszt had to content himself with *behaving* like a nobleman. He started to wear fancy clothes,[18] he let his hair grow until it reached his shoulders, and he walked onstage with all sorts of medals and decorations dangling from his coat lapel. At some con-

---

raised some eyebrows by eloping with Marie, but otherwise found no reason "to cause him to be suspected of holding revolutionary opinions. He rather appears," added the police minister, "to be simply a vain and frivolous young man who affects the fantastic manners of the French. Apart from his merits as an artist, he is of no significance."

[18] At one point he was traveling with three hundred and sixty different ties.

certs he would have garlands and wreaths strewn around the piano, or he might casually toss his doeskin gloves on the ground before beginning his first piece.[19]

AND THEN HE WROTE

Touching upon the career of Franz Liszt as a composer is a problem for me because I don't know where to start. Liszt wrote well over a thousand different pieces, and on top of that, when he wasn't writing his own music Liszt was rewriting other people's, like Mozart arias, Schubert songs, and all the Beethoven Symphonies.[20] A lot of his music was romantic, of course. The Liszt list includes an opera called *The Castle of Love,* a song called "The Song of Love" and a piano piece called "The Dream of Love." [21] Just to make sure he touched all bases, Liszt also made piano transcriptions of Mendelssohn's "Wedding March" and the Bridal Scene from Wagner's *Lohengrin.* Other Liszt inventions were the tone poem, which is a kind of mini-symphony that tells a story, and the rhapsody, which is a kind of tone poem that doesn't. The most

---

[19] He became pretty uppity, too. He once stopped playing in the middle of a concert because the Czar of Russia was talking too loudly, and he refused to play for Queen Isabella of Spain altogether because court etiquette didn't allow him to be presented to her personally.

[20] These transcriptions were enormously popular, but at a dinner party once, somebody berated him for wasting his time on them instead of composing immortal new works. "Ah, my friend," said Liszt wisely, "if I had only written great symphonies, I couldn't afford to serve you trout and champagne tonight."

[21] Or "Liebestraume." Try the recording by the J. H. Squire Celeste Octet.

popular Liszt compositions are probably the Hungarian Rhapsodies, based on Gypsy themes and styles.[22]

ROUND TWO

In 1847, Liszt decided to give up his hectic life as a concertizing pianist and settle down in the city of Weimar, where he could spend more time composing. Before taking up his new position as conductor and musical director at the Grand Ducal Court, however, he made one final, triumphal tour of Russia. And there, in Kiev, he met the second great love of his life. This was Her Serene Highness, the Princess Carolyne Jeanne Elisabeth von Sayn-Wittgenstein, and like Marie d'Agoult before her, Carolyne didn't waste any time in inviting Liszt to spend the weekend at her place.[23] Naturally, he accepted, and found himself at the princess' palace in Woronence, which she shared with her ten-year old daughter and the thirty thousand serfs she had inherited from her father. Carolyne had a few quirky habits, like smoking strong cigars and listening to music while sprawled on bearskin rugs, but she was such a refreshing change from all the other run-of-the-mill princesses Liszt had been in touch

---

[22] He wrote about twenty of them, and orderly as he was, called them Rhapsody no. 1, Rhapsody no. 2, Rhapsody no. 3, and so forth.

[23] "I kiss your hands and kneel before you," the princess wrote in one of her many letters to Liszt, "prostrating my forehead to your feet to assure you that my whole mind, all the breadth of my spirit, all my heart exist only to love you. I adore you, dear Masterpiece of God—so beautiful, so perfect, so made to be cherished, adored and loved to death and madness." They don't write letters like that any more.

with, that he invited her to move in with him at Weimar.
It took almost a year, but eventually Carolyne got permission to leave Russia and she joined Liszt in Weimar,
where everybody was happy for about twelve years.

BUSIER BY THE DOZEN

It was an incredibly productive twelve years. For a while,
Liszt and Carolyne lived in separate quarters to keep up
appearances, but then he simply moved into her villa,
adding his collection of swords, silver breakfast trays, and
pipes to her collection of oriental tables, rugs, and cigars.[24]
There, Liszt studied and taught and composed many of
his most important works, including the dozen tone poems
he dedicated to Carolyne, the Hungarian Rhapsodies, the
Faust and Dante Symphonies, and the marvelous Piano
Sonata in B Minor. Meanwhile, he was also busy preparing and conducting the German premieres of such mile-
stone masterpieces as Berlioz' *Symphonie Fantastique*
and Wagner's *Lohengrin,* plus a whole roster of operas
and symphonic scores by the likes of Schubert, Schumann,
Mozart, and Beethoven. I'm not sure how impressed we
would be today by Liszt's performing forces,[25] but unquestionably he put his stamp on a whole generation of
composers and pianists.

---

[24] Even after the move, the court pretended that Liszt wasn't there,
and continued to address all official communications to him at
his former room in the Erbprinz Hotel.

[25] He put on Wagner's *Tannhäuser* with a tinkly little orchestra of
thirty-seven, and Berlioz once described his chorus as "a lot of
wretches squalling out of tune and out of time."

WEDDING BELLS?

As he neared his fiftieth birthday, Liszt made two major resolves; one was to leave the court at Weimar, the other to marry Carolyne, whose divorce decree had finally come through from Russia. They went to Rome for the ceremony and the Church of San Carlo was hung with flowers when, at the very last moment, as if in a scene from a bad opera, a messenger rushed in at midnight to say that there were complications in the decree. The wedding could not go on after all. There are those who say that Liszt heaved a great sigh of relief at that point, and I wouldn't be surprised. As he told a friend, "I am certain that the best thing for me is to keep my freedom—it is dangerous to bind me either to one person or to one place." On the other hand, Carolyne, who had always been a little on the eccentric side anyway, really flipped. She withdrew into total isolation, filled her apartment to smothering with plants, palms, and flowers, sealed up all the windows, and issued an edict to the effect that under no circumstances was fresh air to be admitted.[26] And there, by candlelight, in a swirl of cigar smoke, Carolyne spent her last years writing a book. It was in twenty-four volumes, of more than a thousand pages each, and it was entitled *The Interior Causes of the Exterior Weakness of the Church.*[27]

---

[26] Even Liszt had to wait outside in an anteroom for at least fifteen minutes before he was allowed to enter the apartment, to make sure he was properly de-ventilated.

[27] No comment.

ABBÉ LISZT

Within a few years, Liszt himself had turned to religious thought and he actually studied for the priesthood, receiving four of the seven decrees on April 25, 1865. At one point he lived in the Vatican, and then later moved into the monastery of Santa Francesca Romana. He doesn't seem to have been anything like your typical abbé, though. We have reports that he would start each day properly with prayers and meditation, but his routine became less and less strict as the hours went along. By evening he was ready to enjoy good company and wine, and even to entertain his friends at the piano. Soon he began traveling again—to Florence, to Munich, to Budapest—and Abbé or no Abbé, Franz Liszt still loved the ladies. He had a nice time comforting the recently widowed Princess Gortschakoff, for instance, and then in 1869 he became ensnared in the charms of Olga Janina. They had quite a tempestuous romance,[28] but when Liszt grew tired of her, Olga blew her stack, as they say. She tracked him down to his hideaway in the Villa d'Este. Gaining admittance disguised as a gardenboy, she planned to stab him to death if he didn't make love to her.[29] Later she threatened Liszt with a revolver, and on yet another occasion she tried to poison him, only to wind up swallowing the stuff herself by mistake. Luckily she recovered

---

[28] Somebody asked Olga if she had ever read the Biblical "Song of Songs" aloud to Liszt. "No," she replied. "The Abbé prefers the real thing."

[29] Fortunately, Liszt did what came naturally, so Olga put the knife away.

after two days in a coma, figured it wasn't worth the trouble, and disappeared forever.

FINALE

In his last years, Liszt was deeply revered as one of the world's most inspiring teachers. His list of students included such celebrities-to-be as Bizet, Saint-Saens, Albeniz, and Smetana. I am proudly aware, by the way, that one of my own piano teachers, Frederic Lamond, was one of those Liszt proteges. Liszt also continued composing until the very end, and he never lost his magic at the keyboard. When he visited London again, in February 1886, only a few months before his death, he inserted an ad in the papers saying that he had come purely as a guest, not a performer.[30] Nonetheless, he couldn't resist playing a few numbers at various parties and soirees, and everyone agreed that his powers had not diminished. Among the appreciative listeners was Queen Victoria, at Windsor Castle. It was a fitting conclusion to the career of Franz Liszt, who never did realize his goal of being ennobled, yet was universally hailed as the king of pianists. "My mission will be to have introduced poetry into piano music with some brilliance," he said. "You see, my piano is for me what his ship is to a sailor; more indeed: it is my very self, my mother tongue, my life."

---

[30] "My fingers are seventy-five years old," said Liszt, "and Saint-Saens and Rubinstein play my compositions much better than my dilapidated self."

"In comparison with Liszt," was Anton Rubinstein's reply, "the rest of us are children."

Chapter Ten
FREDERIC CHOPIN

If Franz Liszt was the undisputed king of keyboard virtuosos, his friend Frederic Chopin became the peerless
poet of the piano. He made the instrument sing, he gave
it new sounds and shadings, and after a short life of only
thirty-nine years, he left us a legacy of masterpieces for
the piano that the whole world adores.[1]

EARLY CONFUSION
Chopin was born in the little village of Zelazowa Wola,
about twenty-eight miles from Warsaw, on March 1, 1810.
At least he told everybody he was born on March 1. The
Chopin biography by M. A. Szulc says March 2, the one
by Fetis has it as February 8, and the birth registry in the
village parish reads February 22, which is the date you'll
find listed in most other music books. *Grove's Dictionary*
has an interesting theory about the mix-up. The reason

---

[1] Almost the whole world. In 1833, Berlin critic Ludwig Rellstab
complained that "Chopin is altogether indefatigable in his search
for ear-rending dissonances, torturous transitions, and repugnant
contortions of melody and rhythm."

the parish registry is wrong, it says, is that the people
there made a mistake when they entered the information.[2]
Incidentally, the baby wasn't really Frederic Chopin at
all. In Polish, his name was Fryderyk Franciszek Szopen.

HAPPY CHILDHOOD

Chopin's family wasn't rich, but they weren't poor either,
and Frederic grew up in a contented home. His father
played the flute and violin, his mother sang, his older
sister played the piano, and whenever they made music
together, little Frederic would burst into tears. Since he
was too young to be a critic, everybody got very worried,
but it turned out that the boy was simply crying with
pleasure at the beautiful sounds. Before long he was picking out tunes on the piano, and at the age of six he went
around the corner to study with a local teacher named
Adalbert Zwyny, who taught Chopin to love Bach and
Mozart. By his eighth birthday, Frederic was good enough
to cause a sensation by playing a difficult piano concerto
at a benefit concert, and already he was starting to write
little marches and a polonaise or two. Royalty took notice
of the prodigy, so Frederic found himself entertaining
counts, princes, grand dukes, and even the Czar of Russia,
who came to Warsaw one day to see how things were.[3]
Chopin played for the czar on an aeolopantalon,[4] and the

---

[2] That'll do it every time.

[3] They were terrible.

[4] As everybody knows, the aeolopantalon was a combination of the
aeolomelodicon and the fortepiano.

czar gave Chopin a diamond ring, which seemed like a fair enough exchange.

SCHOOL DAYS

When Zwyny felt that he had nothing more to teach Chopin, he passed the lad along to Josef Elsner, a well known composer who had founded the Warsaw Conservatory. Elsner realized that he was dealing with a genius, so he guided Chopin without forcing him to follow any rigid rules. "Leave him in peace," he advised one of his colleagues; "if his method is out of the ordinary, so is his talent." Chopin wasn't studying all the time, of course. He was also busy falling in love with a pretty soprano at the Conservatory named Konstantsya Gladkowska. He was too shy to say anything about his feelings, so he just mooned over her a lot, and poured his passion into the gorgeous slow movement of the F Minor Concerto. Chopin's F Minor is called the Piano Concerto no. 2, by the way, even though it was written before the E Minor, which is called the Piano Concerto no. 1. This is because Chopin lost the orchestral parts to the First Concerto (no. 1), and when he finally found time to recopy them, the Second Concerto (no. 1) had already been published.[5]

POST GRADUATE COURSE

When Chopin finished at the conservatory, he was ready to go out into the world and make his fortune. It took him quite a while to muster the courage to leave home,

---

[5] Good that Chopin never wrote a Piano Concerto no. 3 or we'd be here all night.

but since Warsaw had not much more to offer in the way of musical stimulation, and Konstantsya wasn't much help in the non-musical department, there wasn't much point in staying any longer. So he gave his farewell concert in Warsaw on October 11, 1830, and soon afterward left Poland forever, traveling to Vienna, London, Breslau, and finally the city where he would spend the rest of his life, Paris. In each place his music and his playing caused a stir and brought in flattering bouquets of rave reviews. Particularly well received were the *Don Giovanni Variations,* which prompted Schumann's famous salute "Hats off, gentlemen, a genius!" and led another German critic to publish a ten-page review analyzing the score bar by bar, and finding in it all sorts of things that the composer hadn't put there. "I could die laughing at his imagination," Chopin wrote to a friend. "In the fifth bar of the Adagio, he declares that Don Giovanni kisses Zerlina on the D-flat. Where do you suppose her D-flat is?" [6]

SCALED DOWN

Perhaps Chopin might have attempted to continue building a virtuoso's career for himself, but he quickly realized that his tone was too intimate and his playing too sensitive to excite listeners in a large hall. Besides, crowds scared him to death. "I am not fitted to give concerts,"

---

[6] Ever afterward, Chopin used that key as a code word, as in a letter he sent to a lady who had evidently been distracting him rather pleasantly "Who knows what ballades or polonaises have been forever engulfed in your little D-flat major," he wrote. "You are filled with music, and pregnant with my compositions."

he said to Liszt. "The audience intimidates me, I feel choked by its breath, paralyzed by its curious glances, struck dumb by all those strange faces." [7] On the other hand, Chopin found himself entirely at home in the elegant salons of Paris, with their aristocratic surroundings and the sophisticated company of famous artists, writers, and other musicians. Let the critics complain about his too-delicate piano sound in the concert hall—in the salons, it was ravishing. "This is my way of playing," he said frankly, "and it also delights the ladies." [8] The deeper Chopin entered into the fashionable world of Parisian high society, the more he began living the part. He used perfumed handkerchiefs, he had his soft leather gloves made-to-order, he wore silk shirts, velvet waistcoats, patent-leather boots, a long double-breasted overcoat, and a black cape lined with gray satin. He even hired his own horse and carriage, complete with liveried coachman.

PARTY FAVORS

Before long, Chopin found himself in such demand that he could have attended a different soirée every night of

---

[7] The popular virtuoso pianist Friedrich Kalkbrenner offered to cure Chopin's abominable habits and turn him into "something very special" if only he would take lessons every day for three years. Chopin said, no thank you.

[8] When Chopin went to hear Marie Blahetka, whom he described as the leading woman pianist in Vienna, he came away disappointed. "She thumps frightfully," he said, presumably referring to her piano playing.

the week, and sometimes he did.[9] His studio was now crowded with students, many of them members of the titled nobility, and with the money pouring in, he could now afford to give up almost all of his public concerts. He also stopped composing for orchestra, since he no longer had to provide himself concertos to play. In fact, all through his life, Chopin never wrote an opera or an oratorio, not once tried his hand at a symphony, and didn't even attempt a string quartet. Yes, the piano was his only chosen medium. But needless to say, at the keyboard he created one masterpiece after another, many of them cast in the dance forms he remembered from his childhood in Poland—mazurkas, waltzes, polonaises. Usually, Chopin stayed up into the early hours of the morning to write his music, but before that, you could often find him enjoying the Parisian night life, dining with countesses, baronesses, and princesses, hobnobbing with generals, painters, and scientists.[10]

LOVE LIFE

Chopin's social position may have been improving all the time, but his romantic status was no better than it had

---

[9] At one, the hostess was upset that he had only favored the company with a single short piece. "Is that all you're going to play?" she pleaded. "But madame," Chopin answered, with a deep bow, "I ate so little."

[10] One of them was Julian Ursin Niemcewicz, who had a distinguished career as historian, poet, novelist, and president of the Royal Society of Science, but predicted to Chopin that he, Niemcewicz, would be remembered only as a footnote in the composer's biography. Pretty smart fellow, Niemcewicz.

been back in Poland. He had one brief taste "of the forbidden fruit," as he described it, with a "tender-hearted young lady" named Teresa,[11] and he flirted with a lot of his pretty pupils, but nothing even remotely interesting happened until he had been in Paris for at least four years. That was when he met a lovely and talented singer, the Countess Delphine Potocka. They started having lots of dinner together, then they spent hours in deep conversation,[12] and at last they made beautiful music together. "I love her," Chopin admitted in a letter to his family, later going so far as to replace Konstantsya's name with Delphine's in the dedication of his F Minor Piano Concerto. He also dedicated to her one of the most famous quickies in music, the "Minute" Waltz.[13] The next year, Delphine's husband got jealous and made her leave Paris, so poor Chopin had to start looking around all over again. A few months afterward, he proposed to one of his former students, Marie Wodzinska, but nothing came out of that relationship either, except a few letters.[14] In fact, it was not until 1836, when he was twenty-six, that Chopin finally met the real love of his life.

LET GEORGE DO IT

It was at one of Franz Liszt's soirées that Chopin met Amadine Aurore Lucile Dupin, the Baroness Dudevant,

---

[11] Fortunately the doctor was able to cure him.

[12] Her husband didn't understand her, she said.

[13] Eighteen guesses what key it's in.

[14] "At the moment, I'm reading Heine's *Deutschland*," said Marie, in one of her more passionate moments. "It's awfully interesting."

although you could just call her George Sand. For Chopin, it was hate at first sight. "What an unattractive, unpleasant person," he complained to a friend as they walked home. "I'm inclined to doubt that she is really a woman at all." George Sand was very much a woman! It's just that sometimes it was hard to tell, because she wore trousers and a man's top hat, preached socialism and free love, and sat around chain-smoking big cigars. Nowadays that wouldn't seem unusual at all (except maybe the top hat), but remember that this was almost one hundred fifty years ago, and a lot of men simply couldn't get over it.[15] On the other hand, lots of other men got over it fine, which is why George Sand's list of lovers contained some of the most famous writers, poets, painters, philosophers, and musicians in Europe, including Prosper Mérimée, the author of *Carmen*, Alfred de Musset, the French poet, and possibly even Franz Liszt himself.[16]

SAND OF TIME
George must have been one of the busiest women in history. She wrote more than sixty novels, plus all sorts of other articles, papers, stories, biographies, and something like nineteen thousand letters. In between, she took long-distance hikes, climbed mountains, and soaked herself in

---

[15] The celebrated novelist Gustave Flaubert said about George Sand that "one needed to know her as I knew her to realize how much of the feminine there was in this great man." Oh well, his novels are pretty confusing too.

[16] Sand admitted spending a few weekends together with the pianist at her country home, but she kept insisting nothing happened. "Liszt?" she pouted. "I'd rather eat spinach."

the river at dawn, hanging up her clothes on a tree and then lying "with the water up to my chin, smoking a cigar and looking at the reflection of the moon around my knees." Even after she came out of the water, men were always clustering around her, and she chose one after the other in her search for the perfect lover. She didn't believe in wasting time, either. When her divorce decree from Baron Dudevant was being finalized, she ran off with the lawyers who brought in the papers, and her romance with Alfred de Musset ended much the same way—the writer got sick one day and George eloped with the doctor.[17] Under the circumstances, it was remarkable that her love for Chopin lasted a good ten years. She called him "Chop" or sometimes "Chip-Chip." She threw elegant parties for his musical friends, she nursed him through his bouts with various illnesses, and most of all she was his inspiration as he wrote many of his most eloquent compositions.

FINALE

Chopin's final years were difficult, his always frail health giving way frequently, yet he never lost his magic at the piano. In 1848, the year before his death, he went to England and Scotland, giving private lessons, public concerts, and even playing for Queen Victoria.[18] He hated

---

[17] Later, she wrote a novel about the whole affair titled *She and He,* which got Musset's brother, Paul, so angry that he wrote his own version of the romance called *He and She.* Whereupon, one of Albert de Musset's other mistresses wrote still another book on the subject, called *Him.*

[18] That was a waste of time. When she went to write about the

the fog, and the Scottish autumn aggravated his illness, but he faced it with undiminished humor. "Every creature here seems to have a screw loose," he wrote home to his family. "In the castle of one of the most highly regarded great ladies, right after my piano playing, they brought in a kind of accordion and she began with the utmost gravity to play on it the most atrocious tunes. Another sang a romance, standing up as she accompanied herself on the piano; somebody else was whistling to a guitar. They all look at their hands, and play the wrong notes with much feeling. Eccentric people, God help them!" At one of his last concerts Chopin was already desperately sick, but he played a nocturne, the Barcarolle, an etude, the Berceuse, three movements of his Cello Sonata, plus a few preludes and mazurkas, and even the Waltz in D-flat. It was like the musical story of his life. "There was no volume beyond a mezzo-forte," wrote one member of the enthralled audience, "but the sorceries were woven among infinite gradations of piano and pianissimo. Again and again, in the flower-filled room, they called Chopin back until he repeated the waltz, holding himself to the effort by fierce expenditure of will."

CODA
So that's the story of Frederic Chopin, the greatest friend the piano ever had. Many years earlier, just after his arrival in Paris, the twenty-one-year old Chopin already

---

evening in her journal, the Queen couldn't remember his name. "There was some pretty music," she said, "and some pianist playing. The rooms looked quite beautiful."

sensed his destiny. "To be a great composer requires immense experience," he wrote to Elsner, his old teacher in Warsaw, "but nothing can deprive me of the idea and the determination to create a new world." He did precisely that, of course, and Chopin's world of poetry is still explored today by everybody who has ever sat down at the piano—from superstar virtuosos down to first-year beginners.[19] Chopin had a few odd superstitions, like not counting the strokes of a church bell and never entering a room with the left foot first,[20] but his music was made of magic. His nocturnes and preludes, his ballades and impromptus, will live on so long as we have pianists to play them, and listeners with hearts and ears to hear them. And that's here on Earth. "Our dear angelic Chopin," wrote the famous French painter, Ferdinand Delacroix, "must at this very moment be charming the celestial spheres."

---

[19] Old Rellstab, the carping critic from Berlin (see footnote no. 1), had a warning for keyboard students. "Those who have twisted fingers may be able to cure them by practicing Chopin's Etudes," he wrote, "but everybody else better stay away from them, at least unless they have a surgeon handy."

[20] He couldn't go to sleep unless his slippers were lying exactly parallel in front of the bed.

Chapter Eleven
A FLOCK OF FIDDLERS

Ambrose Bierce once defined the violin as "an instrument which tries to tickle human ears by the friction of a horse's tail on the entrails of a cat," and Charles Dickens grumbled that a fiddler tunes "like fifty stomachaches." What did they know? The violin is one of the most beautiful instruments ever designed, and even though most players have to take it on the chin, in the hands of a true artist, it sings like nothing else on earth. Unfortunately, it also sounds like nothing else on earth when the kid next door scrapes away at it.[1]

ROMAN CANDLES
The first famous fiddler in history was the Emperor Nero, but since the violin hadn't been invented yet, he had to accompany the burning of Rome by fiddling on a fidicula,

---

[1] In 1888, four prisoners in a Colorado jail sawed off a portion of the windowcasing in their cell and escaped, while an accomplice was sawing away on a fiddle. The warden later explained that he couldn't tell the difference between the sounds of the fiddle and the hacksaw.

which was a kind of lyre. They say that Nero started the fire himself because he needed a suitable backdrop for his concert (he was also going to recite the story of the Fall of Troy), and it sounds just like him. I am reluctant to be nasty about another musician, but what is there good to say about Nero? The best I can think of is that he didn't murder his mother until he was twenty-two. On top of everything else, Nero was a third-rate lyre-player, only nobody had the courage to tell him so. He sang too, and played the flute, organ, and bagpipe, all equally badly. In 67 A.D., Nero reached the height of his musical achievement when he went to Greece and performed in the Olympic Games.[2] That his soldiers were standing with drawn swords right near the judges had nothing to do with his winning all those prizes.

Who hasn't heard of all the silly things prima donnas do to protect their voices? Well, they have nothing on Nero. The emperor used to lie flat on his back with a plate of lead on his stomach because he thought it would improve his breathing, and he even hired a special voice-officer to follow him around all day to make sure he didn't strain his larynx. If the emperor persisted in talking too much, the officer had instructions to stuff a cloth into the imperial mouth.[3] Otherwise, Nero was just your average, everyday emperor. He lived quietly with his pet ape and a 120-foot-high statue of himself in his simple palace that

---

[2] Nobody had heard of Moscow then.

[3] That sounds to me like a gag.

was a mile long, with a revolving banquet room, walls hung with gold and jewels, and bedrooms fitted out with machines that squirted perfume in all directions. There is no information about how long he practiced the fidicula every day, but his last words were, "What an artist the world is losing in me."

ENTER THE VIOLIN

We know the world survived the loss of Nero pretty well, even if it did take more than five hundred years for another famous fiddler to come along. That's because the violin itself didn't emerge until the sixteenth century. One would think that an important development like building the first violin would have been big news, but people in the sixteenth century had better things to worry about. In any event, absolutely nobody seemed to notice when the violin was invented, or by whom. A number of early instrument makers, such as Caspar Tieffenbrucker of Füssen, are sometimes given the credit, but it doesn't seem likely.[4] Other experts have named Balthasar de Beaujoyeulx as the inventor, but most encyclopedias say no, he was merely the first known virtuoso on the violin. He also may have been the first composer for the violin. As ballet master to King Henry III of France, Beaujoyeulx was asked to prepare a dance for the wedding of

----

[4] Caspar was afraid that his customers wouldn't be able to pronounce such a great long name, so when he opened his lute-making shop, he changed it. To Gaspard Duiffoprugcar.

the queen's sister, and the earliest surviving manuscript of violin music is from this "Ballet de la Reine." [5]

CHAPTER TWO

If nobody knows *who* invented the violin, everybody knows who built the best ones, because the names of these master craftsmen—Amati, Stradivari, Bergonzi, del Gesu—are still magic to this very day, and their violins, dating from the 1500s, have never yet been equaled. Oddly enough, all lived and worked in two tiny neighboring towns in Italy—Brescia and Cremona. For nearly two hundred years they produced one extraordinary instrument after another, and the secret of their success died with them. What was that secret? [6] Modern violin makers have taken old instruments apart and analyzed every measurement, they've even used X-ray devices to calibrate the precise thickness of the varnish, and then they've built new instruments to those exact specifications. It's no use. They produce excellent violins, but they simply can't duplicate the magic touch of those original master craftsmen. In fact, many seventeenth century fiddles get richer sounding as they grow older; they also get a little more temperamental. One English expert claimed that

---

[5] The King said don't stint yourself, so Beaujoyeulx didn't. The wedding ballet lasted more than five hours, included a procession of chariots carrying sirens and tritons with tails of gold, called for hundreds of singers, dancers, and musicians, and was said to cost more than three million francs. I wonder what they did for Bar Mitzvahs.

[6] Well, if we knew the answer, it wouldn't be a secret any more.

his Strad got seasick crossing the Channel and needed two weeks to recover fully.[7] The Viennese violinist Joseph Wechsberg traded in his Amati because it "disliked bright lights," only to wind up with a Strad that "is allergic to smoke, especially cigar smoke, and doesn't like protracted fog, either." In his book, *The Glory of the Violin*, Mr. Wechsberg says that old violins are like young women: "They want to be wooed and may lovingly respond to your efforts, but if you make a mistake, they scream."[8] The great Belgian violinist-composer Henri Vieuxtemps came to the same conclusion. "Never lend your wife or your violin," he advised a friend, "both are sure to come back damaged."

A CARRIAGE FOR CORELLI

Since the best violins in the world were now readily available, it remained only to find first-rate performers to play them, and first-rate composers to write music for them. Arcangelo Corelli was the most important in a long line of violinist-composers who proved that both elements could develop in the same person. Born in 1653, he was the youngest child of an aristocratic Italian family. His two brothers became noblemen,[9] and all his life Arc-

---

[7] Captain Cook, the famous explorer, evidently never ran into that problem. He always carried a violin with him on shipboard, and made his sailors dance hornpipes to keep in trim.

[8] A violin has an hourglass figure, with a curved waist, an arched belly, a graceful neck, a resonating body, and even a cute little tailpiece, so we ought to agree with Mr. W.

[9] Eventually Corelli was ennobled too, but he never fully appreciated the honor. He had already died by then.

angelo was a member in good standing of Roman high society. He conducted concerts at the palace of Queen Christina of Sweden,[10] and performed his own sonatas and concertos at many other European courts. Corelli was something of a miser, wearing shabby clothes and refusing to ride in a carriage unless somebody else was paying for it. He also had a few strange habits, like turning red and rolling his eyeballs when he played. Still, he was the first genuine virtuoso composer for the violin, so we have to make allowances.

A TRILL FOR TARTINI

Giuseppe Tartini, on the other hand, was more emotional off stage than on, and while Corelli was named for an angel, Tartini's most famous work took him to the devil. He came from a wealthy and prominent Florentine family, which wasn't nearly as much of an advantage as you might have thought. You see, even though Tartini had played the violin from earliest childhood, his parents didn't consider music a lofty enough profession, so they gave him the choice of becoming a priest or going into his father's business.[11] Since Giuseppe didn't think too highly of either idea, he disappeared to Padua instead, enrolling at the university there. He told everybody he was studying law, but spent most of his time dueling and fiddling. He became such an expert swordsman that he thought seriously

---

[10] It really would take too long to explain why the Swedish Queen had her Palace in Rome. But that's where it was.

[11] Among other enterprises, papa was an Inspector of the Public Salt Works.

of opening a fencing school in Naples, and he turned into such a fine violinist that no less a personage than the Cardinal of Padua hired him to give lessons to his niece, Elisabetta. In very short order, the gigue was up, Elisabetta and Giuseppe fiddling so passionately that they had to get married. When the cardinal found out, he was livid and gave orders for Tartini to be arrested. Poor Giuseppe had to sneak out of Padua disguised as a monk, and went to hide in the Monastery of Saint Francis at Assisi. There he sat for awhile, practicing his violin and waiting for the cardinal to let him come out. It took two years.[12]

FIENDISH FIND

So Tartini returned to Padua, where Elisabetta had been waiting for him, and they lived happily ever after. For a few months, anyhow. After that, Tartini decided that he had to practice some more, so he left his wife and went off to Ancona, saying he'd be right back. Sure enough, in another couple of years, he was.[13] Meanwhile, it turned out that Tartini's stay in the monastery had been profitable after all. Not only had he invented clever ways to make the fiddle strings thicker and the bow lighter, but he had written one of the most devilishly difficult violin pieces ever known. That happened one night when Tartini began dreaming that the devil came into his room. Quickly they struck up a deal, Tartini signing over his soul in return for having all of his wishes granted. His

---

[12] Some people can't be rushed.

[13] See footnote no. 12.

first wish was for the devil to play something on the violin, and as he said later, "I heard him play a sonata of such exquisite beauty that I felt enraptured, transported, enchanted, breathless." Awakening with a start, Tartini grabbed his fiddle, played as much as he could remember of the piece, then copied it into his celebrated *Devil's Trill* Sonata.[14]

STRINGING ALONG

After Corelli and Tartini, a long parade of violinist-composers came along and made the fiddle one of the most popular of all concert instruments. Possibly the cheers and applause began to turn their heads, though, because each turned out odder than the next. We can start with Tartini's pupil Pietro Nardini, who used to get his violin all wet by weeping at the beauty of his own playing, and Corelli's student Francesco Geminiani, who sold paintings on the side, and once got tossed into the clink for selling one that didn't quite belong to him.[15] Then there was Ole Bull, who wrote a "Quartet for One Violin,"[16] and Franz Clement, who messed up the premiere of Beethoven's Violin Concerto by inserting one of his own com-

---

[14] The devil also fiddled in the film version of *The Devil and Daniel Webster,* but he must have been a little out of practice by then. They called him Scratch.

[15] A lot of violinists had odd jobs: Viotti was a wine merchant, Locatelli was a part-time string salesman, and Beriot used to pick up a little extra cash by insisting that all his students purchase their violins through him.

[16] Ole was the oldest of a lot of Bulls: nine brothers and sisters.

positions in between the first and second movements.[17] Ludwig Spohr was an excellent violinist, but he made his wife switch from the fiddle to the harp because he didn't think the fiddle was a suitable instrument for a lady to play in public. He also felt it was undignified for her to tune the harp on stage, with everybody looking, so he used to do it for her.[18]

SNEAKING ALONG

The list of famous fiddlers also includes a lot of wise guys. When August Wilhemj was selling one of his violins, for instance, he would demonstrate it with a magnificent performance, but when he wanted to buy somebody else's, he made it sound scratchy and full of flaws.[19] Eduard Reményi wasn't above pulling a fast one now and then. On his American tours, Reményi used to astonish his audiences by seeming to draw a full, clear, low note from the violin while at the same time playing difficult runs on the upper strings. It was only when he returned home to Europe that he admitted it had really been an organist, hidden at a backstage console, who had been holding down that mysterious note.

---

[17] He played it on one string, with the fiddle held upside down.

[18] According to Spohr's autobiography, the most famous violinist in Russia at the time was called "Crazy Tietz."

[19] A London society lady once invited Wilhemj to a tea party, slyly adding a P.S.: "Please bring your violin." Wilhemj accepted immediately, only he added a P.S. of his own: "My violin begs to be excused—it never drinks tea." This anecdote has been attributed to other famous violinists, but Wilhemj is the one that counts.

MODERN TIMES

Into our own century, the cavalcade of characters continued, Pablo de Sarasate didn't trust checks and therefore demanded payment in cash after every concert; [20] Mischa Elman was about to return to the stage for a final encore at one of his afternoon concerts, when his father (who handled all the younger Elman's money matters) tugged on his sleeve. "Play this one quick, Mischa," he urged, "the bank is closing soon." Then there was Bronislaw Huberman, the Polish virtuoso who carried a little notebook on all his tours, showing the numbers of the quietest rooms in the hotels he had visited. Whenever he found himself stuck in a new place, Huberman would spend the first night walking up and down the corridors in his pajamas, making notes about the location of elevators or any other noise-producing objects. Sometimes hotel sounds can travel the other way, of course. The incomparable Heifetz was once practicing very late at night, when a woman in the adjoining room called up to complain. "But madame," he said, "I am Jascha Heifetz and I'm preparing for tomorrow's concert." "I don't care if you're Lawrence Welk," she snapped back, "I want to get some sleep!" [21] More in the eccentric department? Yehudi

---

[20] He would stuff the money in his fiddle case and carry it with him wherever he went.

[21] During one of his concerts in London, Heifetz played for the King and Queen of England, who were seated in a loge. At one point, the queen smiled at him, so naturally he smiled back. The next morning, a messenger from Buckingham Palace arrived to inform the violinst that the king wished to see him. "All right, I'll go," said Heifetz, "but believe me, she smiled at me first!"

Menuhin stands on his head every day, and Nathan Milstein insists on walking around the right side of lampposts, never the left. Szymon Goldberg once stopped in the middle of a concert, asked for a wrench, and proceeded to fix a backstage toilet that wouldn't stop flushing.

KING KREISLER

There's a famous story about Mischa Elman and Jascha Heifetz. One time when they were dining together, a waiter brought a letter to the table addressed only to "The Greatest Violinist in the World." Each gallantly insisted that the note must be intended for the other, but when they finally opened the envelope, the letter began "Dear Mr. Kreisler . . ." Nobody who ever heard Fritz Kreisler can ever forget the silky smoothness of his tone and the elegance of his manner, but offstage he enjoyed a joke with the best of them. Once he was strolling along the street of a little New England town when he passed a fish store, with rows of cod on display, their mouths open, their eyes staring. "That reminds me," he said, "I have a concert to give tonight." Like Wilhemj, Kreisler sometimes had to put social climbers in their place. In Chicago, when a rather snooty lady asked him to play at one of her parties, Kreisler demanded a then hefty fee of three thousand dollars. She agreed, then added one stipulation. "I hope you understand," she said, "that you are not to mingle with my guests." "In that case," Kreisler replied, "my fee is only *two* thousand dollars." Kreisler was also a bit of a practical joker, although one experience in Amsterdam cured him, at least for a while. Having a few hours free after a rehearsal at the Concertgebouw, Kreisler went for a walk through the city. When he passed a pawnshop with several fiddles in the window, he playfully decided to see what he would be offered for his precious Guarneri. The owner took a look, asked to be excused for a moment, then suddenly returned with a policeman. "Arrest this man," he said, "he has stolen Fritz Kreisler's violin." Since he had left his passport at the hotel, there was only one way for Kreisler to prove his identity. He took the fiddle out of the case, and bowed the opening phrase of the Mendelssohn Concerto. "He's right," admitted the pawnshop owner, "nobody but Kreisler could play that beautifully." One of Kreisler's pet stories on himself concerned the time a stranger came up to him in a restaurant, having asked the waiter who the familiar-looking man was. "I'm one of your greatest admirers," she gushed. "In fact, I ride in one of your cars every day." So Fritz Kreisler dutifully signed "with kind regards, Walter P. Chrysler."

WINDING UP

That's a fair portion about the violin, and some of the marvelous musicians who've played it. For centuries, experts have been trying to improve on this perfect instrument; they have given us tin violins, aluminum violins, electric violins, and even violins made out of wooden shoes.[22] P. J. Brambach patented a fiddle with bent iron nails instead of strings, and Charles Stroh invented one with a trumpet bell attached. Fiddles have been painted,

---

[22] In his private collection, Jascha Heifetz has a violin made of 2,750 matches glued together.

bejeweled, and inlaid, they've been coated with ivory and bronze, they've been decorated with scrolls, angel heads, and carved mermaids.[23] A certain Professor Wauters, of Binghamton, N.Y., even came up with an automatic violin-playing machine.[24] Well, let them try. No matter what marvels our space age continues to show us, no matter how often we walk on the moon or send cameras to Jupiter, no human can better the incredible achievements of those modest, simple, dedicated men, working under a hot Italian sun all those hundreds of years ago. They, and only they (as George Eliot put it, in a poem called "Stradivarius"), "made perfect violins, the needed paths for inspiration and high mastery."

---

[23] Thomas Jefferson had an American eagle, thirteen stars and his initials painted in gold on his violin bow.

[24] I just happen to have an article from *Scientific American* magazine of December, 1907 about the machine. It printed a diagram of the bowing mechanism, and explained in simple language just how the contraption worked: "When the lever (D) is swung into operative position by the pneumatic (E), the pulley (F) is brought into contact with a driving pulley (G) and is set in motion by a frictional contact therewith. This motion is communicated to the disks (C) which are mounted in the ends of the levers (D) and connected to the pneumatics (E). When one of the bow ducts is uncovered, it operates a valve which deflates its respective pneumatic (E) thus swinging the lever (D) and bringing the disk (C) into contact with the selected string (B)." That ought to do it.

Chapter Twelve
NICCOLO PAGANINI

There must be some who've never heard of the legendary violin virtuoso Niccolo Paganini. Paganini had trouble right from the start. For one thing, he was born in a run-down house on the Street of the Black Cat, and he never did get used to people crossing his path. This was in the city of Genoa, by the way, near Christopher Columbus' house, only a stone's throw away.[1] Niccolo's father, Antonio, loved to play the mandolin, so every evening, he'd go down to the local tavern, order chianti and fried octopus and accompany his friends as they sang their serenades and bawdy ballads.[2] His father worked at the dockyards and the difficulty started when Antonio decided to teach little Niccolo the mandolin, and the kid threw a tantrum every time papa made a mistake. Now we all know of children who are sensitive to music, but Niccolo went a bit around the bend. He would burst into sobs of ecstasy at the sound of cathedral bells, and when he heard the

---

[1] If you have a very strong arm!

[2] Anything, I guess, to keep his mind off the fried octopus.

organ in church, his body would tremble all over and
become bathed in perspiration. Once, when he was five,
he borrowed his brother's violin and got so excited that
he fainted and went into a trance for two whole days.[8]

FIRST FIDDLE
After the fainting incident they kept Niccolo away from
the violin, but he kept pestering and finally, when he was
seven, papa gave him his first lesson. His father had no
ear and even sang out of tune. Niccolo was so talented
that within a month or two he could play rings around
the old man. Suddenly Antonio got a brainstorm. Maybe
Niccolo could become a child prodigy, like Mozart, and
then the family would get very rich, and Antonio could
go straight to the tavern instead of wasting all that time
at the dockyards. From then on it was no more nice guy.
He put the boy into an incredibly severe training schedule, locking him up in his room all day, and beating him
or taking away his supper if he hadn't practiced well
enough. Even when he did practice well enough Niccolo
felt ridiculous, because then papa would stand him up on
the dining room table, surrounded by cakes and sweets,
and make him take a bow to the whole family.

Niccolo obviously hated the whole process, but he
did love the violin, and his progress was fantastic. Within
a year, he had composed his first sonata, played his first
concerto in the Cathedral of San Lorenzo, and was getting
ready for his recital debut. Several local members of the

---

[8] On my word of honor.

nobility were so impressed that they gave the family money so that Niccolo could travel to better teachers in other cities. But his father always went along, nagging, threatening, and pestering. As Niccolo said many years later, throughout his teens he could think of only two things: to perfect his violin technique and to escape his father's control.

FIDDLE FADDLE
Eventually Niccolo reached both goals. He practiced up to eleven hours a day until there was nothing he couldn't fiddle. Then, after winning a local contest and getting a job as a theater violinist, he ran away from home. He also discovered wine, women, and gambling,[4] and vowed to make enough money to support his pursuit of all of them. His first grand passion was for a mysterious noblewoman who took him away to her castle in Tuscany and kept him there for two years.[5] When he left, he gave her a souvenir. It was a "Duetto Amoroso" for violin and guitar in nine movements, subtitled "Entreaties," "Consent," "Satisfaction," and so on.

NICE WORK
IF YOU CAN GET IT
Paganini's next job was as a staff musician in Lucca at the court of Napoleon's sister, Marie Elisa Bonaparte, Princess of Lucca. He conducted the court orchestra, played

---

[4] Perhaps not in that order.

[5] She was teaching him the guitar, he said.

his own compositions at the royal musicales, gave violin lessons to the Princess' husband, and could often be heard practicing in her private bedroom.[6] Sometimes Marie Elisa would swoon from delight while Paganini was playing his concerts. After they carried her out, he was not immune to other ladies of the court.

LADIES MAN

There's no getting away from it. Paganini liked the ladies, and they adored him. "I am not handsome," he admitted, "but when women hear me play, they come crawling to my feet." Since that's exactly where he wanted them, he played a lot. In Lucca, he paid a visit to a maiden at midnight, but entered the wrong apartment by mistake and had to escape by jumping out the window. In Milan, Paganini also entered a wrong apartment, but he found a glorious young woman sick in bed. This time he stayed and said he was the doctor.[7] In Turin, he became infatuated with a fourteen-year old girl, but her father wouldn't let her marry him,[8] and in Genoa, he was actually arrested on a charge of having seduced a tailor's daughter with promises of a wedding to come. "Oh well," he said philosophically, "one cannot always expect to be successful in quests of this delicate nature." There were several other times when Paganini was close to marriage,

---

[6] Before long, Paganini was promoted to Captain of the Royal Bodyguard.

[7] By his third visit, she was all cured.

[8] Papa said he'd think about it when she grew up.

but something always happened at the last minute. "Liberty is a man's most precious possession," he wrote to a friend, and so he remained a bachelor. He liked it better that way.[9]

MUSIC MAESTRO

Meanwhile, the most important development was that Paganini had indeed become the most fantastic fiddler of all time, even if he said so himself. As the great virtuoso, he could use his violin to imitate dogs barking, geese honking, crickets chirping, and rusty hinges squealing. Once he began a concert by making his violin say "good evening" so realistically that the whole audience called out "good evening" back to him.[10] Another time, a jealous violinist made a bet that his rival couldn't sight-read a difficult new concerto. Paganini did it perfectly, making it even more demanding by turning the music upside down on the stand! [11] If a string snapped while he was playing he didn't stop to fix it, he just refingered everything on the spot so that he could get through the rest of the music on the remaining three strings. For one of his girl friends he composed a "Scene Amoureuse" on two strings,[12] and he used to play a number of his most famous pieces on a single string all the way through. In France, the members

[9] So did his son.

[10] Of course, the conversation was in Italian, which is a little easier on the violin.

[11] Aha, using some of my material!

[12] The E and the She, I suppose.

of an orchestra refused to accompany Paganini in a concerto because they were embarrassed at their inability to keep up with his fast tempos. In England, a famous violinist named Mori was so overwhelmed by Paganini's playing that he raised his own fiddle over his head and offered to sell it for eighteen cents. In Italy, Meyerbeer got so excited about his virtuosity that the composer stopped working on the production of one of his own operas, and instead followed Paganini to his next eighteen concerts. In Austria, Schubert borrowed money to hear Paganini and left the concert "as in a trance," while in Poland, Chopin said he was "completely overcome with emotion." "Had he played like that a century ago," wrote one French critic, "he would have been burned as a sorcerer."

MORE TROUBLES

Unfortunately, some people thought they *were* living in the previous century, and they came to the conclusion that to enable Paganini to play so incredibly, there had to be something supernatural about him. Rumors went flying all over Europe: that Paganini had developed his fabulous technique because while in prison for eight years, he spent all his time there practicing; that he wrote all those pieces for a single string because that was the only one on his fiddle the jailer would allow him; that the souls of his mistresses were locked inside his violin; that he could play such fast staccatos [13] because his bow

---

[13] There they are again!

was filled with small leaden bullets; that his tone was so haunting because the fiddle strings had been spun from the intestines of his murdered rivals; and that he was the offspring of Satan, or the very least, he had sold his soul to the devil, who in return guided his every move on stage. Paganini actually had to publish a letter from his mother to prove that he had human parents, and he took out long advertisements in the newspapers to deny the other absurd charges. But people had their doubts just the same. An English violinist tried so desperately to learn the truth about Paganini's virtuosity that he followed him around for six months, eavesdropping on his conversations and making notes of what food he ate. Once, in a hotel, he even managed to get a room adjacent to Paganini's and watched the virtuoso through the keyhole.[14]

MORE TRIUMPHS

As the mystery deepened and the legends grew, Paganini became more and more of a superstar. Empresses, archdukes, and princes fought over the best seats to his concerts, and poor musicians sold their clothes in order to be able to buy the cheaper seats.[15] Admirers would line the streets all the way from the hotel to the concert hall, hoping to catch a glimpse of the great man, and when they could, people would poke at him as though to make sure he was real. He was wined and dined, and at one concert he was presented with a huge wreath by six

---

[14] He probably learned a lot that way!

[15] Quite a sight with the naked people in the cheaper seats!

"virgins of honor." [16] Enterprising businessmen made small fortunes selling "Paganini" fans and "Paganini" perfumes and "Paganini" snuffboxes, walking sticks, buttons, and heaven knows what else. You could eat "Paganini" pretzels and marzipan "Paganinis" and rolls baked in the shape of little violins. A brilliant stroke at billiards became known as "La Paganini," and gloves were embroidered with a fiddle on the left hand, a bow on the right. Paganini became a baron, a commander, a Chevalier of the Golden Spur. They say that in Vienna, an Italian taxi driver who carried the famous artist for a few blocks in his cab appealed to his countryman for permission to let that fact be known. Paganini agreed, the driver painted "Paganini's Fiacre" in big letters on his rig, and was soon in such demand that he could quit cab-driving and buy a hotel with the profits.

MONEY MATTERS

Paganini wasn't losing money, either. Giving concert after concert, he usually insisted that the ticket prices be doubled or tripled. In Prague, he demanded (and received) five times the usual rate. When a cabdriver overcharged Paganini to take him from his hotel to the hall, he explained, "You charge more than that for a place at your concert." "I'll give it to you," Paganini snapped, "when you drive me there on one wheel." [17] Soon his fees were the highest ever paid to a musician, and he was

---

[16] Probably just a title.

[17] Get it?

busier than ever.[18] By now new rumors circulated: Paganini was the stingiest man in Europe. He had more gold than the kings. The only thing he wanted from his audiences was their cash. In some places, he was nicknamed "Paganiente" ("Pay Nothing"). Even so famous and scholarly a poet as Heinrich Heine called Paganini "a vampire with a violin, who would suck, if not the blood from our hearts, at least the money from our pockets." [19] Whatever people thought about Paganini's private life, though, and however much they grumbled about the costs to hear him, they flocked to his concerts and all agreed that his playing was supernatural.[20] "Let mothers, newly delivered, bring their babes to the hall," advised a French critic, "so that sixty years hence, they may boast that they once heard Paganini."

FINALE

That was Niccolo Paganini. Not necessarily the sweetest kid on the block, but certainly the best fiddler under any roof. Also the most suspicious. He kept most of his solo music hidden, so it couldn't be stolen and used by other players, and he always collected the orchestra parts to his concertos so they couldn't be copied. He wouldn't even

---

[18] In Breslau, they offered him so much money that he agreed to appear at an orchestral program, where he played his solos between the four movements of Beethoven's Fifth Symphony.

[19] Nice fellow, Heine.

[20] Perhaps, almost everybody. Sir Thomas Moore complained that his harmonics "sound like the mewlings of an expiring cat."

play his cadenzas through at rehearsals and was pretty tricky in other ways, also. For instance, when he was performing his First Violin Concerto, which is in the key of D Major, he would announce it as a concerto in E-flat, a fiendishly difficult key for violinists to play in. Naturally, everybody was doubly dumbfounded at all the stunts he could do. Everybody but Paganini, that is. He had merely tuned his four violin strings a half tone higher than the rest of the instruments in the orchestra (and so was actually playing in the original key except that it sounded a half-tone higher, or, as he said, in E-flat).[21] Paganini also claimed to have a secret method of practicing. He said it "would enable a young player to achieve in three years the same degree of perfection which, by ordinary methods, would entail ten years of drudgery." Nobody ever did learn that one either, which is why there has never been another Paganini. People have tried all sorts of explanations of his genius, and lately, modern medical experts have been suggesting even more fantastic theories, such as the one reported in *The New York Times* of July 1, 1979. It maintains that Paganini could do all those stunts with the fiddle because he suffered from Marfans Syndrome, and therefore had "hypermobile joints." Maybe we should just admit that he was the one and only Paganini, and leave it at that. Anybody who could say, as he did, that what he wanted most out of life was "a quiet retreat where we can enjoy our musical duets and eat our ravioli," is a man of principle.

---

[21] Well, all's fair in love, war, and fooling the critics.

Chapter Thirteen
ENDS AND ODDS

Here we are, then, almost at the end of our musical travels together, and I have all sorts of odd facts left over. Since it may take a while before I begin writing another book, I shall add some informational bits and pieces, at no extra charge. They're in no special order, and prove nothing in particular, except that musicians may be just as nutty as everybody else.

———————

JEAN SIBELIUS was really named Johan, but his uncle Jean, a sea captain, once left behind some visiting cards by mistake. Always the frugal type, Sibelius began using them and, by the time the supply ran out, he decided to stay Jean indefinitely.

———————

ANTONIN DVOŘÁK was a train freak. Even as a respected professor in Prague, he would go down to the station every day, talking to engineers, porters, guards, and ticket-takers. He knew all the timetables by heart and if a train was late he would run up and apologize to the passengers. On the other hand, Dvořák was terrified by thunderstorms. When one occurred, he would call off his lessons and sit at the piano trying to drown out the noise by hitting loud chords.

———

ANTON FILTZ, an eighteenth century German cellist and composer, devised his own method for cooking spiders, insisting they tasted like strawberries. He died in 1760. The diagnosis: spider-poisoning.

———

CHARLES GOUNOD liked to compose with a large tub of water under his writing table. "When I've been working for an hour or so, my head gets very hot," he said, "and the only way of securing relief is by putting my feet in very cold water."

———

RICHARD STRAUSS had his publisher sue a composer named Heinrich Noren for using melodies from Strauss' tone poem *Ein Heldenleben* in an orchestral suite called "Kaleidoscope." On May 2, 1908, the Superior Tribunal in Leipzig rejected the claim, on the grounds that *Ein Heldenleben* did not have any melodies!!

———

On lawsuits: IGOR STRAVINSKY once sued Warner Brothers for ten thousand dollars because they made a movie in which a girl was seduced to the strains of his

Firebird music. The case was tried in a Paris court, however, and evidently the judges didn't see anything wrong with seduction, with or without music. Stravinsky was awarded one franc in damages.

The English conductor SIR LANDON RONALD once changed Mendelssohn's *Midsummer Night's Dream* Overture to Wagner's *Tannhauser* on a symphony program because a visiting orchestra had recently played the Mendelssohn in the same hall. By the time the concert took place, Ronald forgot about the switch, and when he gave the Mendelssohn downbeat and the orchestra started playing Wagner, he fainted. "It was like treading on a stair that wasn't there," he explained afterward.

Another mix-up story happened on a tour, conducted by FRITZ REINER. The orchestra had been alternating between *La Mer* and *Don Juan,* and on this particular evening, one of the players got confused and started the wrong piece. Afterward, Reiner called the offender to one side, and said he was fired. "But Maestro," the man complained, "that's the kind of mistake anybody could make on a long tour." "Oh, it's not that at all," Reiner snapped back. "It's the way you played it!"

As a young man I was organist at the Western Cemetery in Copenhagen. To add a personal touch to the service I would inquire from family or friends what music had been the favorite of the deceased. Then, during the sermon, I would improvise on a theme or two from that music, just as the eulogy would draw on the deceased's life experiences. Once, a famous singer was to sing a Danish folksong. Due to a traffic delay I arrived at the chapel just in time to play the introduction to the first choir selection after which the solo was to be sung. With no rehearsal I then intoned the lovely song but had had no time to ask the singer which of the two melodies (for the same verse) she had chosen. Of course she began singing the other one—we stopped, glanced at each other—then she switched . . . and so did I!!!

Pianist OSCAR LEVANT once talked himself out of a speeding ticket by explaining to the policeman that he had been listening to a concert on his car radio. "You can't possibly hear the last movement of Beethoven's Seventh, and go slow," he said.

Conversely, another pianist almost talked himself *into* trouble. It happened in Montevideo, when JOSE ITURBI was annoyed by an elegantly dressed lady in the center box who kept fussing with her program, coughing continuously, and keeping up a running conversation with her escort. Finally Iturbi couldn't stand it any more. He went to the front of the stage, bowed, pointed to the loge, and said, "The concert, I believe, is there." The lady retreated into frozen silence, and the pianist continued his recital. Afterward the manager rushed backstage, full of admiration and praise. "What courage," he cried, "to dare to speak that way to the president's wife!"

―――――――

Conductor LEOPOLD STOKOWSKI was often bothered by coughers and sneezers in his audiences. Once, when he was about to start a six-month leave of absence from the Philadelphia Orchestra, he turned to the audience and said: "Goodbye for a long time. I hope that when I come back, your colds will all be better." Stokowski also proposed to the women's committee of the orchestra that all applause be banned. "When you see a beautiful painting or stand before a statue," he said, "whether you like it or not, you neither applaud nor hiss." The committee actually took a vote on the question, the pro-clapping faction winning out by a count of 710 to 199.

―――――――

Fortunately that's one battle I'm glad Stokowski lost, because applause is activated by a feeling of sharing. For the short while we are here it's good to be able to enjoy the beauty in the world and in each other. Performing is for me most gratifying because I am allowed to transmit my sense of contentment and joy to others, and the greatest reward is a spontaneous and audible reaction from the audience . . . especially since most of the rest goes to the government.

A Helpful Glossary
of Musical Borgefinitions

ABSOLUTE PITCH: completely dark
A CAPPELLA: just two, please
ACCELERANDO: hurry up, the conductor skipped
a page
ADAGIO MOLTO: thick shake
AL FINE: all's well
APPOGGIATURA: sorry, wrong number
ASSAI: just assai told you
BAGATELLE: the lady speaks
BAROQUE: butterfingers
CANON: like a round, only louder
CANTOR: late famous comedian
DA CAPO: from the top, only no mistakes this time
DIMINISHED FIFTH: bottoms up
FAGOTT: no, a bassoon
FIFE: two before seven
FIGURED BASS: female baritone
MARCH: between February and April
MINNESINGER: harmonic minor
OBOE: a cockney tramp
ORGAN: vital part of the musician

PIZZICATO: one with tomato, hold the cheese
PONTICELLO: a papal cello
PRIMA DONNA ASSOLUTA: stupid soprano
RECITATIVE: the tune will be along any minute
ROUND: like a canon, only smoother
TRIO: one too many
TRIANGLE: by mutual agreement
UNACCOMPANIED: the orchestra is on strike